THE ART OF MEDICINE

by

FREDERICK W. HAHN, JR., M.D.

Dear Dick & Pat,   January 2006
  Dick, such a great pose deserves
a copy of this little offering. Where
has the time gone? Those were
truly the good old days. I would
like to do a sequel of the practice
years — but we will have to
wait and see about that.

                    Fred (+ marge)

ISBN 1-58597-349-1

Library of Congress Control Number: 2005936400

4500 College Blvd.
Overland Park, KS 66211
1/888/888-7696
www.leatherspublishing.com

ACKNOWLEDGMENTS

I first wish to thank all of the patients who offered themselves and their quest for wellness to my medical education. An indigent patient whom I thanked after I completed a student's history and physical examination on him stated, "I appreciate the good health care I get here at the university. I have no money to pay for this care. If I can offer my body and my illnesses to assist in the education of new doctors, I feel I have contributed something."

I greatly appreciate the role models in medicine who not only cared for me in my youth, but also provided me the incentive to acquire a M.D.

Although I paid tuition congruous to the cost of living during my years of education, the major players in furnishing the fine institutions, instructors and equipment during my years of training were the taxpayers in those states and the nation. These contributions furnished multiples of any dollar amounts I could ever afford.

I must thank the outstanding cadre of dedicated educators at the University of Iowa, Kansas City General and Mayo Clinic who staffed these great institutions. Many, although not mentioned, were recognized nationally and world-wide for their expertise.

Then there are the many I have to thank for their part in putting this collage of memorable experiences together in book/biography form. These date back over a decade when the thought of putting a book together first entered my mind and I started saving notes in a file.

After collecting memories of educational incidences for some time, I first turned to my friend and previous editor, Jessica Palmer, who typed, edited and assembled a simple binding of my initial collection. This provided the encouragement to add to the collection and to one day complete the effort. Her boss and my friend, the late Rodger Yarrington, similarly scanned the early material and encouraged me to move ahead.

Pam Coulter, my office assistant, enthusiastically typed numerous chapters during the mid-part of the project and continued to prod me on. As I neared retirement, I found a renewed desire to complete the project. My daughter, Kathy, who had read my early offering and commented, "Dad, you have to publish this!," collected the CD and additional handwritten chapters from Jessica and became my driving force to get it done. She typed and revised multiple self-edits on the way to putting it into the 8-1/2x11-inch double-spaced format acceptable to publishers.

I am indebted to Bill Ashley for my many late evening and weekend calls for him to keep my PC, WiFi home network and voice recognition program working so I wouldn't bog down. He was also instrumental in establishing my cover photo.

After being less that happy with a first publisher's contract offering, Vivien Jennings, the owner of Rainy Day Books, deserves a tip of the hat for referring me to our own local Leathers Publishing. Here, I wish to express my gratitude to Mollie Eulitt, the book manager, for talking me through the process and "signing me up," and to Joanne Rice, my experienced editor, who labored with me through this novice's publishing effort.

Lastly, I must not forget to thank my wife, Marge, for putting up with the continual "mess in my study" and time away from household and family activities while this offering of memoirs was being assembled. Perhaps a "thank you" may smooth the way for memoirs from the practice of medicine.

INTRODUCTION

Dad drove our robin's egg blue two-door 1936 Chevrolet at a conservative speed up the low grade gravel road that leveled off at the top next to the northeastern corner of the New Castle School ground. At the far end of this three-acre rectangle sat the one-room New Castle Elementary School. Although the road was wide enough for two cars to pass, the sparse traffic generally allowed everyone to "take their half out of the middle." The two car tracks were thus well packed. Even the light traffic pushed loose gravel to the sides of the road, and this repeatedly had to be pushed back to the middle by the county road graders which systematically tended the gravel roads every three or four weeks.

About halfway up the grade, Dad had to swing out of the beaten path to pull around a familiar battered and rusty one-ton flatbed truck. Outfitted with a battered stock rack, it sat empty along the right-hand side of the road. Under the truck bed, lying in the shade provided, was the form of a man in well-worn, striped overalls.

Dad stopped to check out the circumstances. In a short time he returned to our car and informed my mother that the familiar form beneath the truck was that of R.M., a local farmer well known for his abuse of alcohol. Too tired and confused to continue driving toward home, he sought the nearest shade to sleep off his binge.

R.M. was an interesting study in adaptation. One could uniformly estimate his alcohol level by the speed he "herded" his truck down the country roads. When nearly sober, he moved along at a rate comparable with the rest of the traffic. When he was pretty "tanked," he traveled at a snail's pace. When "skunk drunk," he stopped, crawled under his vehicle and slept it off.

That particular sunny weekend afternoon, we journeyed

toward our friends, the Tracys, whose farm was down the road beyond the school. R.M.'s farm was a few sections west and north of his roadside siesta. As one might expect, his farm was run down and minimally productive, but provided an existence to its owner in large part through the generosity of family and neighbors who, when finished with their own cultivating and harvesting, would share in R.M.'s needs.

During my secondary school years, I never heard of a psychiatrist (the only physicians I knew were general practitioners), and alcoholism, rather than a hereditary "disease," was merely considered an excessive lifestyle. Associated or underlying mental health conditions were not a part of our rural vocabulary.

A number of years later R.M.'s barn burned down. Despite "lightning" being given as the cause of the fire, it was justly rumored in the community that careless smoking in an inebriated state was the most likely cause.

As an adult, I was surprised to find that my grandfather in Germany had been an alcoholic. Apparently he was a "functioning" alcoholic, as he worked and provided for his family as a policeman. My father chronicled Grandfather's life as an abusive parent with autocratic tendencies. He described a typical meal as one in which my grandfather assumed his place at the table to eat before anyone else was seated. After he ate his fill, the 11 children could share what was left. If there were two eggs and Grandfather wanted both, the family had none. If he ate one, the family shared the other.

The family lived on a small acreage where my grandmother and the children tended the crops, gardened and cared for the livestock.

When I was of an age that my father felt I would understand, I was told that one night my grandfather went to the shed and was later found hanged to death. I have no clue as to the surroundings of my grandfather's work pressures, health or other mitigating circumstances, other than Dad saying he was a policeman. I must merely assume that he was a very depressed and unhappy man with this state magnified by the abuse of alcohol.

One of my rarely mentioned uncles was merely referred to as the "black sheep." I found that he, too, was given to heavy drinking. He could not hold a lasting marital relationship. Only his drinking was consistent, while his work and social arrangements were short-lived.

As I began to travel and communicate with my relatives in Germany, I found that the substance abuse problem has been one that has penetrated each generation, just as does diabetes or any other hereditary illness.

My First Partner, Art

This brings me to the person (and others like him) for whom this book is dedicated. Art C. became a dear friend when I was a third-year resident at the Mayo Graduate School of Medicine. He was a first-year resident in the same ENT specialty. He was exceedingly bright, cheerful and caring.

What originally impressed me most about Art was that he would always carry his share of the load — and then just a little more. I shared this tendency; therefore, we dove into our work as soul mates, never having to worry about the other carrying his portion of the workload.

While interning in Kansas City, Missouri and "moonlighting" at the Independence Sanitarium and Hospital emergency room, I noted that there was only one ENT physician in Independence and he was nearing retirement. This appeared to be an excellent location to start a practice.

We mutually agreed that I would start in Independence and could count on Art coming to join me at the end of his last two years of training. We kept in touch, and it worked out just that way.

We started out gloriously in a community that opened their arms to each of us, creating a relationship that was warm, friendly, and to my knowledge without ever having hard feelings toward each other. This happy situation progressed for three years.

Then one day an emergency room nurse dropped a hint that really caught me by surprise. She, with a twinkle in her eye, related, "Your partner must have been out to a great party last night!"

"Why?" I asked, knowing that he had been on call.

"He came in to see a patient about 2:00 a.m. and was still pretty tipsy," she volunteered.

Unfortunately this occurrence slowly but steadily became more frequent. Excuses and cover-ups became necessary. He became unreliable for nighttime duty, and the scenario progressed over the ensuing months. Eventually, I had to be available for back-up call in case Art could not be reached at night. At first he brushed this off as not having heard the call, or a variety of other excuses.

Slowly the problem extended into the daytime hours. At times he would not appear at the hospital on time for surgery. I spoke seriously to his private scrub technician about monitoring his ability to carry on and to summarily cancel any case where it appeared that there was going to be a risk to the patient(s).

One of his faithful patients musingly said to me, "Dr. Art is doing surgery on me in the morning. Don't let him drink too much tonight." Our business manager and I spoke to Art frankly, expressing our grave concerns.

Nonetheless, the problem escalated into the midday. Art sometimes would be fine in the morning, leave for lunch, and come back to the office completely incapacitated. The mechanism for this was not clear until he started having single-car accidents. Empty vodka bottles were found in his wrecked cars.

Then one day I found a new, frequently "detailed" tranquilizer lying on the office floor beneath his white coat. We began to believe Art was mixing vodka and the tranquilizer, which accounted for his unbelievable transition in the short period between the beginning and end of his lunch break. Art drove Oldsmobile "Ninety-Eights," which were not unlike "tanks." He seemingly felt safe in them. Three harrowing crashes destroyed the respective cars, but miraculously protected the cargo and confirmed this belief. With the occurrence of noontime transitions escalating, the mechanism was put in place for treatment in the first of three treatment centers. The first was administered by psychologists and geared to treat the patient initially, and then include patient and family members over 12 years of age during the later portion of the course. Art did admirably for about four months; then his old pattern returned.

The second dry-out effort was in an out-of-state facility at Emory University in Atlanta, Georgia. This facility had a treatment program designed specifically for physicians. The dry-out period was followed by the physicians actually caring for subsequent physician patients going through the same process. Again Art responded appropriately for a hopeful four- to five-month period, and then resumed his frightening downward spiral.

Art's final treatment, afforded by our office, followed a serious discussion in which it was suggested that one of two choices must necessarily be followed: either a psychiatrist would be selected to regularly monitor him or, if this was not done, his next fall from the "wagon" would mean termination from the practice. The practice at this time had invited a third physician, Dr. W.M., into the group. He was apprised of the problems before joining us.

Art proclaimed an aversion to psychiatry and elected to manage his problem personally. The inevitable occurred. Art relapsed once more. W.M. and I chose to carry him as an employee long enough for him to be covered by insurance through one more treatment period. This third inpatient treatment effort was set up at the Menninger Clinic, near Topeka, Kansas. Art, knowing that his fate was sealed, left the practice without confrontation or being asked to do so.

Concerned physicians and peers at the University of Kansas ENT Department found him a salaried job at Fort Leavenworth, where he ran the ENT specialty clinic for some time.

Several years passed and he seemed to stabilize. His physician friends in Liberty, Missouri encouraged him to come back to his home community to practice. He tried to reestablish a private practice, with all of us pulling for him and furnishing surgical tools and personal assistance as we could. However, his previous trail of abuse and indiscretions made it difficult for him to acquire appropriate insurance. The difficulties he experienced apparently led to a severe state of depression, and ultimately Art took his own life. Sadly, he left a devoted and charming wife and three bright and talented children.

To this day I repeatedly have people speak with concern about Dr. Art. Most are aware of his outcome; some continue to be shocked and mystified. Patients and peers uniformly had a great respect and love for him.

Personally, I reflect back to a poignant time when I came into the MCI Hospital record room and library. Here one area served the dual purpose as a chart room for patient records to be completed, dictated and signed, as well as a safe storage and reading area for physicians' medical reference books. One evening I came to this room intending to complete my charts. I found Art standing and reading a book. I mentally noted the color of the book and the empty slot on the shelf. After some small talk he left and I checked to see which book he replaced. It was a psychiatry text. I surmised that he was desperately trying to understand his devastating health problem. Retrospectively, I have often wondered if his underlying illness may not have been bipolar (manic-depressive) disease. I have seen others do very well on medication and wonder if today's choices had been available to him at that time, would he still be with us today.

In times past we were often collectively searching for him, hoping he would once more be found safe and unharmed. We only tangentially sensed the pain and frustration experienced by his family. No one can weigh the torment suffered by his wife, mother, children and other family members. No one can truly appreciate the fear and emotional upheaval experienced by his entire family.

The "Art" of medicine encompasses the educational effort to study and understand disease processes we encounter in health care and the effect those disease processes have on the lives of patients and those close to them. The "Art" of medicine involves a continuing search for answers as to how we can best treat those disease processes plaguing both the patient and their significant others. The "Art" of medicine deals with teaching each of us to accept life as it is presented, without excuse or justification, creating a plan and proceeding with hope and determination, while learning from the many lessons of life that are presented to us along the way.

Art is sorely missed by those of us who were patients, friends, acquaintances, associates, and family members. We pray that continued improvements in responding to health care needs, including mental health needs, will furnish relief to those who seek assistance through the "Art" of medicine.

The role we must play as physicians, peers, friends and family is to continue to love and care for those affected with these health needs. For the sake of both patients and society, we must continue to support the academic effort to harness the vast collection of depressive mental health disorders, just as we continually look for improved mechanisms for the treatment of physical impairments.

Art, in receiving his B.S., graduated summa cum laude. He was voted "Most Likely To Succeed" by his alma mater and joined our society as a delightful young professional. We regret that the last window of opportunity to salvage Art passed before an appropriate solution could be found. It is my hope that our professional and social failure in his passing will stimulate a successful conclusion for others.

TABLE OF CONTENTS

■ CHAPTER 1 ■

The Art of Remembering Our Roots

MORE THAN THREE-FOURTHS of a century ago, a young man, who just happened to be my father, corresponded secretly from Esslingen am Neckar, Germany, with his third cousin, John Heide, in rural Fulton, Iowa, USA. This cousin had traveled to the United States as a child with his family before World War I. They settled on a farm near Fulton in eastern Iowa.

Before my grandparents were aware of this correspondence, my father — then 19 years old — made arrangements for John to sponsor his trip to the United States for the price of three years' indentured service on his farm. This arrangement was consummated despite his mother's protests, and Dad came to the United States, along with two other German lads, in 1923. His fiancé was to come but got cold feet at the last minute and, as Dad said, "Couldn't leave her mother."

At the end of his required servant relationship, Dad worked day labor for Clarence and Lydia Campbell. He put all the money he could in the bank in anticipation of one day returning to Germany. Unfortunately, everything was lost in the Great Depression. Later, he rented a small house close to where Mother taught school in a one-room schoolhouse in Fulton, Iowa. They met, dated and were soon married. After marrying, they moved to a small rented farmstead adjoining that of John Heide and owned by Wiley Campbell. I was born in the only downstairs bedroom in this farm home 10 months later, and basically grew up there.

John was decidedly religious and the obvious patriarch of the Heide family. He was responsible for the organization of an RLDS church congregation in June 1888. It was here that my family attended church as I grew up.

John's son Amos, then middle-aged, had a large family that was dispersed widely around the Midwest and beyond. One of John's grandsons, Cleo, lived in Missouri. Every year he and his family would come to visit the farm six miles north of the county seat town, Maquoketa, Iowa. Cleo had a son and daughter, who were slightly older than me. When they came for a summer visit, one of the rituals that I will always remember was the trip to the old "sand ditch."

The "sand ditch" was the product of water erosion in a sandy-soiled portion of the 80-acre pasture on the southern edge of the Heide farm. The "ditch" was the repository of a large accumulation of fossils dislodged from underlying limestone bluffs and many other relics from surface drainage. Frequently Indian-made arrowheads were uncovered by the men plowing in the nearby fields. Others were dislodged in the sand ditch by spring rains. This territory, I understand, had once been inhabited by the Sioux Indians a century or two earlier. This accounted for the name "Maquoketa," given to the longest river running through Iowa and into the Mississippi River. Walking barefoot in the warm sand while concentrating intensely on locating the next worthy object for our cousins' collection was pure and memorable joy that just fit a small lad's fancy. Back at the farmhouse the rock hunt often stimulated John Heide — whom we called Grandpa Heide but was actually my fourth cousin — to bring out his shoebox collection of arrowheads. These had been discovered in the fields as he walked behind a single-bottom plow pulled by a horse.

In November 1945, a few years after my last recollection of our visit to the sand ditch, Grandpa Heide died. After his death, the visits from his grandson and children became less frequent, and eventually only the grandson and wife came to visit. Their children went off to school, married and assumed their own lives.

My secondary school years passed all too quickly, and soon I too left home for my higher education, far away from the farm. The imprint of Grandpa Heide's influence still remains with me and those of us who knew him. Before he died, two of his grandsons who lived in Arkansas and Missouri made an occasional visit back to Iowa. One was a particularly gifted storyteller. Now, some 60 years later, I can still recall him very seriously telling of his encounter with a bear. Wide-eyed, my brother and I listened as he told of the bear chasing him down through the woods, across a meadow and up to the edge of a lake. "In desperation," he said, "I ran out onto a log that extended into the lake. Once on the log, there was no place to escape. I turned around to face the bear just as he attacked. As the bear growled and opened his mouth to grab me, I reached far down into the depths of the bear's throat, grabbed his tail, and jerked so hard I turned the bear inside out, and he ran off the log in the opposite direction." It was several years later, when refocusing on my youthful imagination, that I realized the bear story was truly a fabrication.

After my wife Marge and I were married, school and the military service caused us to move 13 times in as many years. At last, our young family came to the metropolitan Kansas City area to practice medicine. We chose a church congregation nearby. It was only after a number of years attending this church that we accidentally discovered that Pat Taylor, a fellow church member, was the same "seventh" cousin who annually came to the Iowa farm to search for fossils and Indian relics in the sand ditch. A short time and a few conversations later, we learned that the granddaughter of my memorable storytelling sixth cousin, Angela Iles, also attended this same congregation.

On the one hand, third cousins seem to be quite distant. Yet this tie was close enough to draw my father away from his immediate family for the rest of his life. Although the blood line has become widely dispersed, it seemed uniquely strange how those threads are still being woven into the fabric of our lives. The strength of those fibers reinforces the cloth of life from which we have been constructed.

Hidden away somewhere in our attic, I still have one of the arrowheads I was personally fortunate enough to find on Grandpa's farm. The horse and the single-bottom plow are now gone from the old homestead. The outbuildings are in a state of decay. Yet both the arrowhead and the contact with my distant cousins regularly remind me of my father's early determination to succeed in America. I am both proud and amazed at Dad's course of action and marvel at the raw determination that resulted in our collective presence in these United States.

■ CHAPTER 2 ■

The Art of a Good Start

WHILE SEARCHING FOR inspirational material to present at a church service 25 years ago, I ran across an article in a news magazine regarding a research project conducted in California. The article described an educational program where teachers presented one unit of material to a diverse group of students. Those who excelled were then asked to help teach the material to those unable to fully grasp the subject matter. The study resulted in several conclusions.

First, when peers present educational material to slow learners, comprehension dramatically improves in the slow learners. Second, it was apparent that as the more gifted students taught the material, they attained an even greater understanding of that material. At first reading, I thought what a grand piece of research! Then, after a moment of reflection, I recalled fond memories of New Castle Elementary School in Farmers Creek Township, Jackson County, Iowa, 1940 to 1948.

The school was bordered by a weathered wooden fence, constructed of four 1x 8-inch spaced and untreated boards supported by round pine posts every eight feet. New Castle was a tidy white wood-framed, one-room schoolhouse nestled among towering oak trees. It sat next to an east-to-west country road that connected the communities of Andrew to the east and Iron Hill to the west in the rolling hills of eastern Iowa. Twenty paces to the east of the schoolhouse sat a small white shed used for stores of wood and coal. Further east was the clearing large enough for a softball field. Home plate was snuggled up against the back of the coal shed such that the building could function as "pigtail" for the inexperienced catchers. Twenty-five feet south of the coal shed a swing set, including two swings, rings, a chinning bar and two teeter-totters, stood ready for play. Two well-trodden paths coursed along the east side of the schoolhouse and west of the swing set on their way to two tiny white frame outhouses sitting side by side along the wooden fence at the southwest corner of the acreage.

A large iron bell in the belfry on top of the north end of the schoolhouse roof rang a 15-minute warning before school time. When our teacher rang the bell again, 10 minutes later, daw-dlers playing in the field or along the roadway knew they were about to be counted tardy and would receive a checkmark on their grade card if they didn't hurry. The ringing of the bell also marked the end of our lunch hour and the completion of mid-morning and afternoon recesses.

One Room

I remember kicking my boots off on the old boot jack, adding them to the neat row of footwear lining the walls of the anteroom and then walking into the solitary large schoolroom. The only door in the room entered from the anteroom, the latter being little more than a lean-to on the northeast corner of the building. There were shelves in this northeast corner of the schoolroom where our lunch sacks or buckets were placed. Limited shelf space above this and an old metal cabinet ac-commodated nearly half of our reference library.

An immense sectioned slate chalkboard covered the whole front wall of the room and wrapped back two more sections on each side wall. Adequate chalk and erasers were spaced on the chalk rail beneath the blackboard. The teacher's desk and sev-eral straight-backed chairs were the only furnishings at the front of the room.

I would estimate that the ceiling was about 12 feet high. A

Floor Plan of New Castle Elementary School

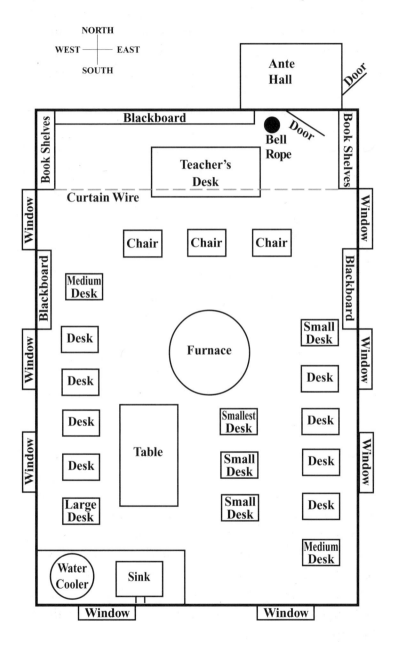

No. 9 wire coursed across the room at the seven-to-eight-foot level as a reminder of where the curtains would hang to transform the front of the room into a stage for Christmas plays and special PTA programs. Numerous framed classic prints were spaced around the front wall above the blackboards and the forward portions of the side walls. One more set of built-in bookcases was located west of the front wall between the blackboard and the first of three windows on each side wall. A rope from the bell tower came down through a hole in the ceiling and was tied to a nail near the floor in the right front of the room just to the west of the door.

A large circular furnace sat near the center of the room providing the only source of heat. On a table in the southwest corner, a five-gallon crock water cooler was perched next to a simple sink that drained onto the ground outside the back wall. A large table used for art projects was positioned on the south central portion of the room. The remainder of the room was filled with neat rows of desks graduated from tot size in the forward portion of the room to ones that could accommodate a muscular eighth grader in the back of the room. The east side of the room accommodated the first four grades, and the west side, the upper grades. The latter contained the inkwells for dip-pens that were no longer in vogue, thus, no further threat to pigtails.

One Teacher

In this single-room schoolhouse all eight grades were taught simultaneously by a talented and seemingly superhuman being. This skillful, female teacher quite adroitly covered the gamut of subjects and grade levels. Early on, board and room for her in one of the parent's homes was the norm. This became less common as transportation improved.

How did she do it? First, she taught the assigned subject matter to each respective class. In those classes with slower

Students and teacher at New Castle. Front row: Mona Kay Tracy, Miss Lucille Irhig, Jimmy Merrick. Second row: Patty Tracy, Jimmy Sutton, Janet McCutcheon, Meredith Garretson, Frederick Hahn, Neil Hahn, Jimmy Rockwell, Donnie Beetle, Rita Rockwell.

learners, she selected one of the better students to help those who had more difficulty grasping the material. Often two or three children comprised a grade level. When there was just one pupil, she resorted to calling on a student from the next higher grade level for assistance.

When the more capable students in one grade level completed their work, they were free to observe the work of the higher grades as they worked at the blackboards or recited at the front of the room. A gifted student could play mental games with themselves by silently trying to answer the question posed to the upper class member reciting at the front of the room before that student could respond. The material taught to the lower classes was reinforcement to that already learned.

One Exceptional Experience

Those of us who attended such one-room schoolhouses have unknowingly endorsed this "new" educational system, described in the above mentioned journal, without benefit of government grants or modern-day research. I am sure there are those who would be amazed at how many of the students educated in such one-room multiple-grade schools have gone on to graduate from a variety of professional schools and have become successful in other than agricultural vocations.

When it comes to education, we may see a steady flow of new tools and techniques. However, I would echo the words of one of my favorite professors, Dr. Kenneth Devine at Mayo Clinic, who frequently repeated the Old Testament statement: "There is nothing new under the sun." Thus, when any person is seized by the desire to join the ranks of the medical profession, or any other profession, he or she need not feel inferior or defeated simply because of a humble educational beginning. That person may have simply been part of a sophisticated educational research project with neither formal design nor funding.

Deficiencies

This primitive educational system did have its deficiencies. One case in point was represented by "Junior." He was a farm boy who first dropped out of school at the third grade level. Each year the superintendent of schools attempted to interrupt Junior's truancy. My last recollection of Junior was when, at 15, he made one last-ditch effort to complete fifth grade.

Junior liked to play softball, which was our major sports activity in the spring and fall. This particular year, armed with a pack of cigarettes in his shirt pocket, he made his academic reentry in the spring. Needless to say, he was always selected early when we chose up sides to play ball.

Team selection itself was a lesson in fairness. Two of the

older students would be chosen by the teacher to "captain" a team. One would toss a ball bat to the other. The receiving captain would catch the bat with one hand. The two captains would then alternately "walk" up the bat hand over hand. The last person whose hand could hold the bat at the top would choose first, and then they would alternately choose their team members until every student had been chosen. Those chosen last necessarily had a lesson in "humble pie."

Junior's last stint in fifth grade lasted six to eight weeks. When he turned 16, the school authorities were no longer required to persist. Junior returned to his farm home where vocational education consisted of on-the-job training (OJT). In an agrarian community this was generally acceptable. Other choices could similarly require no more than OJT.

Sex Education

I might hasten to report that modern sex education was not part of the country school scene. Background knowledge came primarily from each child's farm experience of observing mating and often farrowing, calving and foaling (which was thus part of every rural student's background). As school progressed, sex education classes (at least for boys) were held in the boy's toilet. The male urinal was constructed of wood, as was the bench-like stools (two-holer). Here early heroics included "stream force" measured by maximum heights reached on the front wall splashboard of the latrine.

Stories and sex jargon shared by the upper grade boys were absorbed by the younger boys. At times, the subject matter was too advanced to be grasped by the younger boys. One example I recall specifically was a World War II verse which mixed patriotism and sex, and was verbalized by an eighth grade boy. It went like this:

I lost my arm in the Army;
I lost my leg in the Navy;

I lost my balls in Cedar Falls;
And I lost my cock in a lady.

My brother, then in third grade, tried to memorize the verse and repeated it frequently when we were together on the farm. However, as a third-grader he had some trouble with the concept. Much to my frustration at the time, he would monotonously chant the verse closing with, "I lost my cock 'by' a lady." Feeling compelled to accuracy, I repeatedly corrected him. "No, *in* a lady!" It was truly amazing how much more a fourth-grader understood than did a third-grader.

For all of us who attended New Castle, sex education was matter-of-factly observed through animal husbandry on our respective farms. During school days in the hot Iowa spring and fall seasons, little girls wore thin cotton blouses. Breast development was not a secret and went on quietly except for an occasional jealous comment or grasp of an older girl's development by a younger girl. Menstruation was handled in a totally discreet manner.

The Day of Truancy

One nice spring day, school was canceled for a teacher's meeting, or some such reason. My brother Neil and I agreed, with two sisters who were just about our age, that we would not tell our parents about the holiday, bring our sack lunches to school as usual, and go on a field trip together.

Several miles south of the schoolhouse, there was a bluff 200 to 300 foot in height running above the river bottom next to the North Fork of the Maquoketa River. There were many caves, crevices, and evidences of Native American passage through this same area. Above the bluffs was wooded pastureland. The face of the bluffs was irregular enough that we could climb along various ledges and trails and hypothesize how American Indians had scaled these bluffs long before us. The thrill of the climb was heightened by quandaries as to what we would do if we encountered a rattlesnake — which was not totally unlikely.

After exploring what we all geographically referred to as "The Bluffs," we ate our lunch. At that time we were all between about 11 and 13 years of age. Our hormones were beginning to flow. However, in contrast to the youngsters of today, we were not ready to explore beyond our timid fantasies. We were satisfied to crawl 30 to 35 feet back into a crevice-like cave and cuddle and talk for one to two hours before gathering up and heading back to school and then home.

My brother and I kept our secret, but the girls, concerned their parents would find out through some roundabout turn of fate, spilled the beans. At the next PTA meeting we were exposed. There was a bit of static, but mostly with a wink between parents and with tongue in cheek. That was one of my early educational experiences which thereafter caused me to realize I would be more comfortable just being open and truthful with my parents.

Lessons in Social Graces

Other lessons of social values were learned at this one-room school as well. When fall came and the temperature dropped, the room needed to be heated. As with every other chore, this too was the responsibility of the teacher. When she arrived at school, she had to go to the coal shed, get a bucket of coal, and with a small pile of paper and kindling wood, start a fire in the furnace.

Appreciating what a physical chore this was for one of our favorite teachers, my brother and I explored a way to accomplish the fire-building project before our teacher arrived. We found that we could jimmy the window at the front of the room nearest the woodshed. After crawling through the window, we would unlock the door from the inside, carry in some kindling and a bucket of coal, and get a roaring fire going before the teacher arrived.

Legally, we may have been breaking and entering. However, the good intent of performing a service seemed to have the greater moral value. Thus, the tradition continued from day to day, week to week, year to year and from fall until the warm days of spring made the deed unnecessary.

All in all, our education in a one-room school contained just about all the learning one youth could absorb.

▪ CHAPTER 3 ▪

The Art of Learning from Simplicity

IT IS COMMONLY said that one came from a "humble beginning." Although there is often pride in the distance between that humble beginning and whatever status in life one achieves, the "outhouse" is rarely mentioned as an educational institution. It was often described as a sight of bravery, particularly when it had to be visited at times when the temperatures hovered below zero degrees Fahrenheit (wind chill in those days was not in the vocabulary).

The particular facility my family and I frequented as I grew up was still being utilized when I brought by prospective wife, Marge, to meet my family during the fall of our senior year of college.

Our "outdoor john" was indeed an extension of the similar facility that I described at our country school. However, rather than copying the two-hole design we had at school, ours was a deluxe job with three holes — large, medium and small (just like the three bears — no pun!). It was made of raw, unpainted oak and had a wood-shingle roof. There was a small window high on the back side which faced the chicken house, and this was covered with a screen in the summer and isinglass in the winter. The front door was hinged on the left side, and a large staple held a hook that latched into a second staple on the door jam to the right.

Not to be wasted, my grade school project of the panoramic winter scene I had carefully designed in "art class" covered the upper walls. The background of eight to ten sheets of 8-1/2 x 11-inch light blue construction paper pasted together was decorated with dark green Christmas trees, white snowmen, dark blue birds, children and a dog. It made a continuous ring around the interior of the facility and was held there by thumb tacks. This was the proud product from my one-room New Castle School.

Next to the big hole, there was a roller for Northern Tissue toilet paper. However, more conspicuous than Northern Tissue (which was generally present only for company) were parts of one or more old Sears and Roebuck, Spiegel and Montgomery Ward catalogs. I will confirm that the soft sheets were at times used up, leaving nothing but the dreaded slick pages. Early on, when the catalogs were nearly intact, they were a great source of entertainment and information as to what was available to those with more means than ours, and at a minimum, a great "wish book."

My brother and I found that if we remembered to take some "farmer's matches" with us in the winter, the slick pages could be wadded up, lit with a match, and dropped down the hole to produce heat. Sometimes when other paper already deposited below caught on fire as well, the tiny inferno was enough to cause us to rise up from our annular "throne." The distance below was great enough that the building never did catch on fire.

It was here that we learned to outgrow our fear of the dark. While there was still some question of the "boogieman" being real, our visits to the toilet were accompanied by one of our parents. As we grew older, they were allowed to stand on the wooden plank outside the door, which provided the approach to the toilet, and conversed through the door (often encouraging us to "hurry up"). As we matured, they were allowed to stand just outside the kitchen door and make us aware of their willingness to protect us from the never identified wild animals, such as bears, tigers and wolves, by an occasional brief comment.

About this time in our learning process, we found that there was security in numbers, and my brother and I would, for safety, venture to the "outhouse" together. It is amazing how much better brothers can get along when they have a common adversary — such as fear of the dark and dangerous wild animals.

Eventually, reason did overcome fear, and we began to believe that indeed "there's nothing out there that will hurt you!" That was certainly reasonable, but at times fearful moments would cause us to break into a run on the way back along the 50-foot path to the back door. This bit of uneasiness was at times promoted by periodic mischief, consisting of large rocks thrown against the outside wall by an unsuspected prankster when one was in deep thought and least expecting a deafening blast against the wooden wall.

We learned that if the door was opened just enough to allow a slit of viewing space, the throne could furnish a peep hole (peep slit) to the wonderful world of activities going on near the kitchen door. Such wonderful things happened there, ranging from Mother sitting in the shade snapping beans, an old rooster getting his head cut off on a chopping block and feathers plucked, to a visitor coming to the kitchen door. That caused us to be particularly quiet in our hiding place.

One evening during such an event, the beheaded rooster, which was placed on the ground next to the chopping block, jumped up from his place of execution and ran down the hill by the woodshed and into the garden. The whole family was called out to locate him in the dark.

Quite often I suspected that my brother would find that an announced sudden urge to frequent the outhouse would be a means of avoiding a particular chore which was disliked by all, but mostly by him. A protracted stay seemed to confirm this, but constipation is hard to deny (then again, there was

Best friend Dick in front of "3-holer."

the toy section of the Sears Catalog). There were other hazards to encounter and events which distracted our thoughts away from the boogieman. Among these quite common aggressors were the spiders that enjoyed the cover of a roofed facility. If left unmolested, these creatures sometimes grew to quite a large size. One always feared the dreaded black widow. A peek down the hole before being seated was a must. Once seated, a fly caught in the web up near the roof could furnish considerable visual entertainment as one watched the spider go in for the kill.

Additional friendly protection was offered by both man and boy's best friend, our family dog "du jour." When things seemed particularly scary, just a whistle was all that was needed to get our furry friend to come and lay at our feet. It never seemed to be too much to ask for her to leave her warm gunny sack bed in the woodshed to come and stand guard.

This small three-hole institution held many fond memories. One of my most treasured photographs is one my mother took of my best high school friend, Dick Sagers, and I clowning around in front of this architectural feat.

I sadly relate our outhouse's final deed to society. It occurred during halftime at a Maquoketa High School homecoming game. Long after my parents moved into town and the farm buildings sat vacant, a bunch of high school boys tipped her up and loaded our dearly beloved outhouse onto the back of their pickup truck. They hauled it to one end of the football field and burned it, along with someone else's similar institutional facility, in effigy (or just for plain spite)! Whatever the case may be, I still miss that simple institution and all that I learned within its walls.

■ CHAPTER 4 ■

The Art of Dogging It

ONE DAY WE looked out our kitchen window as Hanna, our neighbor's then young but nearly full-grown Doberman pincher, frolicked in their backyard. As much as we enjoyed her, we, for obvious reasons, always accompanied our small granddaughters when they were playing in our backyard while Hanna ran loose in theirs. The three-foot fence would one day be no challenge for Hanna at all.

As we watched her, I reflected on the many dogs that have played a vital role in my family's life, teaching valuable lessons that one can readily translate into meaningful lessons for our higher animal kingdom.

Buster

The first dog I remember was called Buster. He was an all-white puppy except for bandit-like black markings around his eyes. He was brought to New Castle School as a Christmas present for my brother and me by John Hobson, a strawberry and watermelon farmer who lived a mile west of New Castle School. Buster grew up and became a constant companion and playmate for my brother, Neil, and me.

After truly becoming family, Buster one day turned up missing. His remains were not found along the roadside or anywhere on the farm. His disappearance was the first real "family" loss experienced by my brother and me, and we missed him dearly.

Sister Berta with Buster.

Out in the farm community there were — even at that time more than 60 years ago — older farmsteads that were occupied by more transient folks of questionable ethics. Some of these less tasteful neighborhood folks had admired Buster. They had relatives who lived 20 to 30 miles away, beyond our county seat town and at the edge of the next county. It was always my mother's contention that such a contingency "dog-napped" Buster and took him to their relative's farm. This was a much more acceptable explanation for concerned boys than his being struck by a car.

I was never fully clear how my mother could come to that conclusion, but it was always there as food for thought in conversation with our trusted farming neighbors. While I remember the hurt and associated healing that came with this experience, I also remember a new friend coming into the family.

Pup

She wandered onto our farm as a stray looking for a home. Having no name, she just fondly became known as Pup. While Buster was thought to be a spitz and terrier mix, Pup was a size-and-a-half larger Heinz 57 mixture of collie and whatever breed of dog that was resident in her mother's community.

She was a very loving dog and soon replaced the relationship my brother and I had had with Buster. She, like all of the dogs who came to our farm, had their personal cardboard box lined with a couple of gunny sacks in the woodshed to the south side of the house. She was found outside the kitchen door almost as soon as the door opened. In the summer she would rest next to the door where she would be sure to get the first chance for attention, or food scraps from inside (not necessarily in that order).

As I recall, it was nearly two years from the time that Buster disappeared that Dad, Neil and I were out in the yard near the southeast corner of the house. Here on the south side of the house was a plank walk that led from the concrete deck between the house and the woodshed to a cement cistern. The cistern caught soft water that ran from the eave troughs on the house. This furnished water to do dishes, the washing and bathing. On the side of the plank opposite the house was a very old and very large lilac bush.

I don't recall why we were at this location (unless it was to pump some soft water to take into the house), but I recall that seemingly out of nowhere a little white dog with black markings around his eyes came up to us almost bending in two as he wagged his little behind. Although thin and looking somewhat different than we remembered him, in a few moments we realized this indeed was Buster. For a brief time Pup felt that her territory had been invaded. However, the two dogs soon became great companions. They came to the barn for fresh milk when Dad milked the cows. They lay in the cool sand of the dirt road that wound down a "Rocky Hill" north of the buildings between the house and barn.

Since there was very little traffic in those days, my brother and I often joined the dogs to play in the sand, making roads for our little rubber cars with the damp sand and wooden two-pound cheese boxes. At times, we would build great piles of sand and hollow them out to make sand castles. As we grew older, we shared the commonly held concept that if we could just dig deep enough in that sand, we could go all the way to

China (that's where those kids lived who were poor and starving, and the reason why we always had to clean our plates). Both dogs lived out their years with us. Buster became so senile and deaf that the neighbors would have to stop and honk their horns to get him to move out of the road. I don't remember how he died, but my mother thought that he was finally killed by a car. I'm sure if that was the case, my father cared for him discreetly.

Pup, who was significantly younger, was fond of chasing cars that came down the road. One evening while we were in the barn at milking time, Pup was struck by the Edwards' car while she ran barking and nipping at the tires as the car passed by. She floundered over an embankment to the edge of a small pond at the downstream edge of a large drainage tube running beneath the road. Mortally wounded, we had to go to the house and get the shotgun (which normally was used only to shoot varmints) and put Pup out of her misery.

Lady No. 1

Our next family pet was furnished by another farm neighbor, Duane Tracy. This was a bit larger dog, a mix of collie and shepherd. She was given the name Lady. Like each of the family dogs, she was always given a pan of fresh milk at milking time. However, she first had to follow the etiquette of the barn, which meant that she had to sit quietly until the cats drank their fill. She could then step up and finish the pan (plus get a bit more from my softhearted father if the cats were particular hungry and left too little).

As we grew older, we spent a lot of time at our distant Edwards cousins (John Heide's daughter Nettie and kids) who lived up the hill to the west. We ascended our upwards slanting backyard, took the path through the orchard to the stile that Dad had built over the woven-wire fence leading to the Edwards' cow pasture, skirted their garden and hen house and turned right into their backyard. We very commonly overstayed our expected return home: be it for a meal, chores, or other reasons long since forgotten.

What does ring clearly in my mind is that my mother would step outside the kitchen door of our home and in her very best hog-calling voice shout, "Fred - R - I - C - K" multiple times. Mr. (Pete) Edwards would often be out doing chores or working around the farm buildings while my brother Neil and I were inside visiting or eating "Aunt" Nettie's hot homemade bread smothered with real country butter. He would come into the house relating, "I just heard the wireless."

Of interest is the fact that Lady soon learned to take her position next to Mother, face up the hill towards the Edwards' and immediately follow my mother's call with a shrill "Owoo-o-o-o-o-o." Retrospectively, I'm not sure whether Mother's piercing shrieks hurt Lady's ears or she just enjoyed the duet. Whatever the case, both were effective.

Lady No. 2

Next in the line of canines that came to our house was a puppy from the litter birthed by the same mother who gave us Lady. Lady was growing old and senile. This was to be the mother dog's last litter. She, as you might expect, was called Lady No. 2.

The relationship that Lady No. 2 achieved with my father may have been partially learned from her older half-sister, Lady No. 1. What she did achieve could well be the reason why a dog is spoken of as "man's best friend."

Dad's modus operandi was to feed the hogs and then go to the cow barn, pick up his staff (a shepherd's shaped staff carved from a sapling tree) and proceed into the barnyard. Early on, Dad would walk out of the barnyard through the gap in the barb wire fence and into the 80-acre pasture where the cows grazed. Sometimes they would be at the far end of the pasture.

Dad with Lady II, daughter Debbie, and sister Berta.

At other times, they would have grazed their way back to the top of the hill east of the barnyard.

It was only a short time before Lady No. 2 caught on to what needed to be done. As soon as Dad took his staff and stepped outside of the barn door, Lady No. 2, who always followed close on his heels, would strike out across the pasture and, like a trained Australian sheep dog, bring the cows into the lot without Dad ever leaving the barnyard. She became his constant and faithful companion.

After years of this loyal loving relationship, tragedy struck. When one of Dad's implements broke, he put the broken item on a two-wheel trailer that he pulled along behind his H-Farmall tractor and headed down the road toward Mike Knacksted's farm. Mike had a welding unit and would be happy to repair the broken part.

Lady No. 2 trotted down the road next to the tractor as they approached the neighbor's farm. As they did so, the Knacksted's dogs came out to challenge Dad's and Lady's approach. As they did so, Lady No. 2 shied back and was accidentally caught under the large back wheel of Dad's tractor. The wheel ran up onto her hind quarters before Dad could stop. Needless to say, Dad felt terrible. He put the mortally injured Lady No. 2 on the trailer and hauled her home. He summoned our veterinarian, who determined that her pelvis and hips were fractured. Dad could not bear the initial suggestion of putting her to sleep, but was aware that she would likely die from the injuries. Dad placed Lady No. 2 in the woodshed on her familiar cardboard and gunny-sack bed and left food and water for her. He then went to do his chores.

After getting the cows fed and milked, he came out of the barn to find that Lady No. 2 had dragged herself out of her box in the woodshed, along the plank walk by the cistern, and down the hill to the bridge in front of the garage that led across the road to the barn. This she did by pulling her painfully shattered and useless hind quarters with the strength of her front legs. Despite her mortal injuries, she was determined to be at her master's side to assist him. On his next visit, the veterinarian again pointed out that Lady No. 2 would not likely survive her injuries. Dad acquiesced and allowed him to painlessly relieve Lady of her suffering with I.V. medicine.

Mother still speaks of Dad mourning and being unable to eat for the better part of week. Could one ask for a more poignant lesson on friendship?

Pooch

The last in the list of farm dogs that graced our farmstead was another stray dumped off at our farm. This dog was thin, mangy and displayed the traits of having been severely abused. Although I was off to college by this time, my sister, who was 13 years younger than I, and my father developed a deep friendship for this poor canine as well.

At first, when anyone spoke to this dog, which after a time was labeled Pooch, he would shy back and initially even show his teeth. Particularly through my sister Berta's persistence, he was fed and spoken to kindly until such time that he could be petted and felt confident that he was not going to be abused further.

Like the other dogs, he became my father's constant companion, being nurtured and fed by a fellow proven to be dogs' best friend.

When we were able to find a home in town for my aging parents, they knew the city was no place for a farm dog. My father again grieved severely when a farm family 13 miles away near Bellevue agreed to take Pooch as their farm dog. Dad and Mother went one time to check on Pooch's welfare. Dad felt so badly about him being restrained on a chain and more poorly treated than he had hoped, that he was unable to bring himself to go back to visit again.

As a schoolboy, I learned the following verse written by Edgar Albert Guest. When I think of the wonderful friendships with our many farm dogs, this verse again comes to mind. The first verse states:

A boy and his dog make a glorious pair,
And no better friendship is found anywhere,
For they walk and they talk and they run and they play,
And they have their deep secrets for many a day.
That boy has a friend who thinks and who feels,
Who walks down the road with a dog at his heels.

Perhaps we should just conclude that a dog is both a man's and a boy's best friend.

CHAPTER 5

THE ART OF PLANTING A SEED

SHOW BUSINESS IS a much more limited field than medicine if one considers those who do succeed in providing a livelihood for themselves and their families, and those who do not. The few who attain stardom in show business are duly recognized. In fact, the coined phrase commonly quoted is, "A star is born!" Somewhere in that star's past, someone or something planted a seed that caused them to want to be a star. A physician must have a seed of desire planted as well. This is often at a young age. The seed must then germinate into a strong desire to practice medicine.

It is difficult for me to say exactly when the seed to become a physician was first planted within me. My memory does hold possibilities. It may have been at the tender age of seven or eight during an incident that occurred while riding on an old oats binder.

My brother and I were standing back of the oats binder apron. Ahead of the apron was a sickle blade that mowed down the ripened stalks of oats. The cut stalks then fell onto the apron and were carried along on a moving canvas to the end of the apron where they were collected into a uniform bundle. The bundles were automatically tied with twine and ejected into a bundle collector. After eight or nine bundles accumulated in the rack, it was tripped and the bundles were dropped onto the ground. Soon the bundles would be formed into shocks to dry. Usually seven bundles were set on their butt ends with the grain up. Another bundle was bent in the middle and spread out over the shock to protect the heads of grain as well as to hold the shock together.

On this warm sunny day my brother and I stood on the board framework behind the moving canvas apron and held on to an iron support rod that ran three feet above the back edge of the wooden platform. As we rode along, I absentmindedly swung my foot beneath the board framework. Lurking there was an uncovered steel cogwheel and linked chain system that propelled the apron. I thrust my right foot directly into this cogwheel drive. As my foot was pulled into the wheel, I reflexively gave a quick and mighty jerk. The sudden tug, plus the bulk of my forefoot fortunately was enough to derail the chain. I did sustain a large star-shaped laceration on the top of my foot. For all practical purposes, it was a miracle my entire forefoot was not amputated.

The Seed Is Planted

Paul, my shirttail cousin and grandson of Grandpa Heide, who was about a decade older than I, was operating the bundle drop while his brother Dale drove the tractor that pulled the machine. Paul saw the accident, shouted to Dale to stop the tractor, scooped me up in his arms and at double time carried me across the field to the neighboring farmhouse. There my dirty, wounded foot was soaked in some Epsom salts water while my parents were called and preparations were made for my first trip to Dr. Jordan's office. Dr. Jordan was a solo general practitioner in our county seat town of Maquoketa.

The experience was a memorable one for me. My father and the doctor's nurse held me down while Dr. Jordan administered open-drip ether through a cloth-covered wire mesh mask. After my injured foot was repaired, the trip home was even more memorable. Every few miles I had to have my father stop the car so I could rather violently upchuck along the highway. This incident, plus the follow-up visits, provided my first role model image of the family physician. I believe the care given me by this compassionate practitioner planted within me the first seed to become a doctor.

Once planted, a number of illnesses over the next three or four years fertilized and nourished that tender seedling. As I approached 10 years of age, I had a recurring illness felt to be related to recurrent tonsil infections. Dr. Jordan suggested that my tonsils be removed. My parents, who survived on a very minimal income, definitely far below today's poverty level, discussed the problem of payment with Dr. Jordan. He generously agreed to do the surgery for $25. I can still remember my parents' comments about his compassionate handling of the situation. They were most grateful.

As the date for my surgery was scheduled, I did have some input into the decision regarding the type of anesthetic to be used. After my first experience with ether, I vowed I would do anything to avoid another encounter with this vile anesthetic agent. Even though I was only 10 years old, Dr. Jordan was willing to consider my wishes. He agreed to take my tonsils out under local anesthesia. This was accomplished while I sat in a straight-backed dental chair in his office. The procedure was carried out with seeming ease and was certainly preferable to open-drip ether. I was most appreciative of his sensitivity to the wishes of a child.

My office stay was extended through the night, however, as I continued to hemorrhage throughout the remainder of the day and evening, I was observed in a small examining room that served as a recovery room. His nurse, Eunice Brown, spent the night with my mother and me. Her name seemed easy to remember because she was such a warm, caring person. I remember thinking, "You're nice, Brown." Periodically through the night, Dr. Jordan came in to check on me and to replace the tonsil sponges as necessary. By the next morning the bleeding had subsided and I returned home to the farm.

The Seed Sprouts

The seed began to sprout seriously three years later when Dr. Andrews (the last local M.D. family practitioner to do home deliveries in our community) came to our country farmhouse to deliver my baby sister, a "change of life" gift to the family. He had a working arrangement to take care of Dr. Jordan's deliveries when Dr. Jordan ceased this aspect of medicine.

My mother went into labor the evening of May 14, 1947. Dr. Andrews drove the seven miles from Maquoketa, arriving about 9 p.m. He attended my mother until my sister was born between 3 and 4 a.m.

My parents asked my brother and me to retire early to our bedroom on the second floor of our turn-of-the-century, unimproved farmhouse. However, with all the excitement, we were in no mood to sleep. Even if we had been, we would likely have been kept awake by Dr. Andrews' "piano concert." He opened the piano bench in the sitting room, got out all of my mother's sheet music, and played the piano throughout the majority of my mother's labor.

Occasionally, he would go into the bedroom, which was just off the sitting room, and check on Mother's progress. He then faithfully returned to his piano playing. With habits like this, I could see how a physician could become a skilled pianist.

Brother Neil, sister Berta and Fred.

Our "birthing room" was without plumbing, as was the rest of our home. My father provided a pan of boiled water from the cookstove in the kitchen and a recent edition of our weekly newspaper, the *Sentinel*. The latter was used to protect the bed and dispose of the afterbirth (placenta). Just 13 years earlier, I was delivered in this same primitive suite by another family practitioner, Dr. Lauder, who was a generation older.

This whole birthing scenario perpetuated and deepened my interest in medicine.

The Sapling

About a year later, another personal experience with the medical profession nurtured the sprouting seed within me to grow into a young sapling. My parents had repeatedly badgered me about my slouching posture. I can remember my mother saying, "Straighten up, Frederick. Don't slouch like that." Because of their lack of funds, plus the promises of a local chiropractor, I went every Saturday to have everything popped, from my neck to my hips. He told my parents he could correct my stooped posture with weekly treatments over a year. The weekly adjustments theoretically would correct my kyphosis (hunchback deformity). I remember the dreaded sound of the midsection of the adjustment table being released. This meant a quick thrust of the gentleman's hands down on my back and the series of snaps up and down my spine

Fred with cast for kyphosis.

as the joint facets popped open like a series of small suction cups.

The progressive deformity of juvenile epiphysitis common to rapidly growing teenagers apparently was not part of this gentleman's training or understanding. A simple and appropriate exercise program would more likely have improved this problem. The window of conservative management to correct the problem passed and the deformity worsened.

One day I accompanied my mother to Dr. Jordan's office where my baby sister was being seen for her "well baby" followup. Without comment or request from my mother, he noted my posture. He immediately recognized the problem, and within weeks I had an appointment to see a world-famous specialist (Dr. Steindler) in the Children's Orthopedic Department at the University of Iowa. Dr. Steindler, well-known primarily for his care of the various polio deformities prevalent at that time, assumed my care. After several seven-to-ten-day hospital stays and six months in a body cast, I again assumed a respectable posture.

Although I would like to expound at length about the entire episode leading to acquiring appropriate medical care, suffice it to say that at this juncture I first began to appreciate mainstream medical care.

This was an extremely stressful period for both my parents and me. It likely could have and should have been avoided; however, this exposure to the art of appropriate medical care did cement my desire to become a physician.

A Mature Tree

The subsequent school year was a year during which I had hoped to play football and emulate my senior high school "heroes." Instead, I necessarily turned to public speaking contests, singing and instrumental music. This was not because of my ability to forecast the future, but because Dr. Jordan insisted,

First male cheerleader at Maquokota High — Fred and the girls (Sylvia Dolch, Nancy Stewart, Ruth Waters, Betty Nairn and Florence Ripple).

"No football!" In order to attend athletic games, and not further stress our family budget, I tried out for and became the first male cheerleader at Maquoketa High School.

I progressively began to form the image of what I might become. A sense of direction began to mold this farm boy in ways that could not be fully appreciated until manhood

▪ CHAPTER 6 ▪

The Art of No "What Ifs"

IN THE PREVIOUS chapter I briefly described a period of therapy to treat the kyphosis I experienced as a result of juvenile vertebral epiphysitis (irritation at the junction of growth between cartilage and bone). If this fairly common condition had been recognized and given appropriate treatment (physical therapy) earlier, I might have been spared the discomfort and expense of a more elaborate corrective course of treatment.

In every generation there have been many people who endured unusual hardships and sometimes died prematurely because they lived before technology and prophylactic medicines were available to treat or prevent their health problems.

This was the case for many of the friends I gained during my stays at the University Hospitals in Iowa City, where I went to have my physical deformity corrected. Because I was 13 years old, I was assigned to Ward "B" in the Orthopedic Department (the boys' ward). I was surrounded by young men ravaged by polio. One young man in particular made an indelible impact on me.

Perspective on Life

It was 1947. Frank Smedka, whose home was in Dubuque, Iowa, had severe scoliosis — an S-shaped deformity of the back as the result of polio. On days when I started to feel sorry for myself, I would simply look across the aisle to his corner of the ward and be reminded of what he was enduring.

Instead of wearing a cast from shoulders to hips, as I had

to do, his cast extended from under his chin, preventing him from turning his head without turning his entire body. It was difficult for him to get up and move about. At the same time, it was a challenge to be comfortable sitting or lying down. Comparing Frank's problems with my own always put things back into perspective. I realized that my lot was, comparatively, not so bad.

Frank was about three years older than I was. He had begun the process of formulating philosophies that would carry him into adulthood. He was old enough, and had been at this rehabilitation effort long enough, to be a great help to me.

When one wears a body cast for a number of months without bathing, itching beneath the cast sometimes becomes unbearable. Unable to reach and touch the many areas of his body that itched, Frank discovered ways to relieve the unrelenting torment. He introduced me to the use of a yardstick and loops made by opening wire clothes hangers, which could be introduced down inside the cast. Even then, there were times when one could not reach a particularly itchy spot. In just such situations, he demonstrated an unusual prowess with a simple pocket knife. After boring a hole through the cast over the site that itched, he poured alcohol through the hole onto the troublesome site. This gave amazing relief!

Frank's attitude was always upbeat and positive. He was a wonderful help to me in solving many relatively minor problems. Thankfully, I had no permanent loss of muscle function as he had experienced with polio. I did not have a withered lower limb on one side to cause me constant problems. Yet I can recall his expressions of joy and good cheer. Frank was a terrific role model for ward mates with both lesser and greater challenges than he experienced.

In those days it was quite common to have men and women in iron lungs occupying the private rooms on the ward. Perhaps Frank's more mature awareness caused him to appreciate the fact that he was not relegated to such a miniature submarine-like appearing machine as a requirement for each succeeding breath. Perhaps he had a perspective I was too young to appreciate. Whatever the thought process that occupied Frank's mind, I never heard him ask, "Why me?" or "What if?"

Popeye's Veggie

Having been reared on a meat-and-potatoes farm cuisine, I had no experience with the vast selection of foods that were "good for me." One appearing regularly on the hospital menu was cooked spinach. I had never tasted this delicacy before, and if it were not for the Popeye comic strip my father read to my brother and me when we were small boys, I would have had no awareness of this being an edible food. After my first taste, I realized this was not something I wished to consume. The problem was how to present a clean tray at the end of the meal, as required by our rather militant head nurse on Ward "B."

Frank again came to the rescue. He located a small table on the sun porch that was out of direct view of the nurse's desk. Close to the table was a window pane with one triangular piece of glass missing.

Frank showed those of us junior to him how to spoon unpalatable food through this defect and drop it over the edge of the foundation, while an ambulatory accomplice (patient) positioned himself to watch for an ever-impending visit from the nurse. On the one hand, we each received our daily "attaboy." On the other hand, had Olive Oyle been in danger, none of us would have been able to save her. How appropriate to keep everything so positive in the face of adversity (spinach).

Close Family Friend

My admiration for polio-handicapped persons began a number of years before my personal orthopedic treatment. I attribute this to having met an acquaintance on my mom's side

Frederick and Neil on a visit to Uncle Wilbur at SUI, where Fred would later be a patient.

of the family. Del Donahue was a radio personality who worked at the university radio station in Iowa City, and later transferred to major radio stations in Kansas City and Chicago.

I first met Del when I was about eight years old. He came to visit my mother's brother, Uncle Wilbur, who was hospitalized at the University of Iowa Hospitals. A horse had reared up and fallen back on top of my uncle. Del was paraplegic, "crippled" by polio. He could only move with the assistance of braces on his lower extremities and Canadian crutches. At this tender age, I was very impressed by Del's apparent love and gusto for life, despite his handicap.

I never knew Del well enough to understand how he felt about his handicap. But, as I grew older and had the opportunity to share with other handicapped people like Frank, I began to appreciate how a burning desire to succeed could overcome adversity. Indeed, this determination allowed Del to become a very successful regional radio personality.

Overcoming

Del and Frank had physical handicaps attributed to polio that could have caused them to give up their dreams. Instead, they became proud useful citizens who contributed both physically and attitudinally.

We all have our individual crosses to bear: some physical,

some situational, some great, and some small. Thank goodness for those who have become role models for others by not resigning themselves to failure with a, "What if I had just been whole?"

■ CHAPTER 7 ■

The Art of Closure

AS A YOUNG man, polio was a common household word. It was also a word that brought fear into all families with children and grandchildren. Since little was known about the disease, the fear was even greater. The symptoms started like a sudden bout of the flu, with fever and systemic symptoms, followed quickly by flaccid paralysis of a portion of the victim's body. This sometimes involved the limbs or one side of the body. Commonly, it would involve both lower extremities. When the spinal cord was damaged high in the cervical area and respiratory muscles were involved, the disease often became life-threatening. Without the use of the respiratory muscles (bulbar polio), the person's life could only be sustained with an "Iron Lung."

Particularly fresh in my memory is an experience at the Jackson County, Iowa Fair. With much urging, my father agreed to take my mother, brother and me to the fair. At this interval in the epidemic, both awareness efforts and funds to assist in caring for the disease had become prevalent; Sister Kenny's physical therapy mechanisms and the March of Dimes support were underway.

As part of the awareness and fundraising effort, there was a March of Dimes booth at the fair. For a voluntary contribution, one could walk through the small tent and see a functioning iron lung with a female patient receiving the rhythmic respirations required for life.

I can remember stepping up about three steps to a platform in front of the respirator. Her feet were toward us by the entrance and her head away. Her entire body, except her head, was in the large cylindrical chamber. Much of the top of the respirator, which was hinged like a barbeque barrel, was glass. As we walked by, the bellows compressed air into the chamber, forcing a volume of air into the iron lung. As it did so, some leaked out of a crack in the glass upper half, striking me in the face. I recall my fear that this gust of air would give me the dreaded disease.

The young lady mouthed a thank you for our concern and small contributions to the March of Dimes.

In those early days of the polio epidemics in the United States, public meetings and areas of community concentration, such as municipal swimming pools, were closed in the summer months.

As I noted in Chapter 6, the children's orthopedic wing of the hospital was filled in those days with youngsters having muscle transfer surgeries and construction of orthopedic devices to facilitate ambulation.

It was not until a generation later when our own children were in early elementary school that Drs. Salk and Sabin perfected their vaccines. We were in Iowa City in medical school when there was a citywide effort to immunize with the oral (Sabin) vaccine. A series of tables were set up in the street, and long lines formed with parents bringing children for a small paper cup with a sugar cube impregnated with the limb-saving, and sometimes life-saving, vaccine.

While a fellow at Mayo Clinic in the late '60s, I, along with each of the ENT fellows, cared for a lady who had contracted polio during the last major U.S. outbreak (1952). She had come down with bulbar polio. Her daughter, who became paraplegic, was fitted with Canadian crutches and continued her pursuit of a career at Rice University in Texas. The lady herself, however, was at first relegated to a standard iron lung, and later to a portable iron lung. This was a machine that compressed only the chest cage and was more mobile. By the time I arrived at Mayo, she had been dependent on the portable unit for more than 15 years. She had pneumonia and other acute respiratory episodes frequently enough that a permanent room was finally assigned to her in the pulmonary wing of St. Mary's Hospital.

While she was battling her progressive pulmonary fibrosis and the associated "Chronic Patient Syndrome" related to her prolonged illness, her husband, a department head, developed multiple sclerosis. Happening to be a Jewish man, I can still remember him half-jokingly contemplating that, "God must be an Arab!"

There was an interesting aside to my "Polio Connection." During my stays at the University of Iowa Hospital, I became acquainted with "Cookie," the Chinese kitchen worker who brought the hot food from the kitchen to the orthopedic wards in the children's section of the hospital.

Years later, while early in my practice in Independence, Missouri, I met a Chinese obstetrician. As we compared our medical career patterns, I found he had at one time worked at the University of Iowa Orthopedic Hospitals. Our conversation about my youth and his career course revealed that Dr. Liong had been the "Cookie" who delivered food to the Ward "B" when I was a patient at the University Hospital in Iowa City.

He subsequently went to medical school and then did an OB/GYN residency in St. Louis. He elected not to establish his own practice, but worked out his "late onset" career as an employed first assistant to a well-established obstetric and gynecology group in our community.

CHAPTER 8

■ The Art of Invitation ■

As a high school freshman, my "Ag" teacher, Mr. Noland Zugschwerdt, invited me to write a 10-minute oration and deliver that first original creation from memory in competition. He worked tirelessly on improving my presentation. I won this first local contest, proceeded to the sectional, and finally to the state contest — with his helpful guidance.

This beginning led to my competing in numerous speech contests during my four years of high school. These contests generally started locally at Maquoketa High and progressed to regional and state competitions. Often the competition would be presented in front of an assembly, which included all, or at least a large segment, of the student body.

It was at such an assembly early in my sophomore year that Ms. Eunice Boardman, our local music director, came up to me and complimented me on my presentation. She then proceeded with the following invitation: "You have a nice speaking voice. You should have a nice singing voice as well. I'd like to invite you to come out for men's chorus."

The compliment and accompanying invitation was most welcome. I liked to sing at our small country RLDS Church. In fact, my mother played piano, my father had a nice bass voice, and at times we would provide the so-called "special music" at church services.

As a young man, Dad sang in a community men's choir in Germany. The group, in fact, has been continuous for over a century. They meet in a German pub, learning by rote the music

47

taught to them by a "choir master." After each practice, they socialize in the pub.

Singing was also an integral part of our family's social life. Our family was dear friends with the Tracy family. Mrs. Zana Tracy both read music and "played by ear." Before television, and with little else to do in the evenings in a small rural community, we often got together with neighboring families to visit; usually during the course of the evening we would gather around the piano to sing.

Mr. Tracy was a forceful man who always wanted to have us meet at their home (which was significantly more substantial than ours). He didn't sing, but loved to have our family and other families in the neighborhood gather around their piano and sing through just about all the sheet music they owned. Anyone who had acquired new sheet music would bring it along as well.

The playing and singing included the sheet music of most of the then popular tunes, followed by a large number of favorites from the church hymnal. Often the singing was done in harmony parts. Afterward, the children gathered to play everything from "hide 'n seek" to sharing in youthful talk fests. The adults usually drifted into a game of cards; "7-up" was generally the game of choice, and often lasted beyond the small children's bedtime.

I can particularly recall my brother falling asleep early and having to be carried to the car at the Tracys', into the house once home and encouraged to do the things a little boy has to do to keep from wetting the bed while still half asleep.

This preparation through fun family singing was a major factor leading me to accept Ms. Eunice Broadman's invitation.

The second major ingredient in the musical stew was a girl in our neighborhood, "cousin" Mona Edwards, who lived up the hill from us. She was a cousin six or seven times removed. Mona was a rebel farm girl and also a granddaughter of John

Heide. She would not cut her fingernails and therefore claimed this as an excuse for not participating in milking cows, as her older sister and two brothers were required to do.

Mona loved popular 1940s and '50s music, as I did. In a time and setting where one had to manufacture their way out of boredom, she was a self-taught pianist. After chores and dinner at their home and ours, I would regularly travel up the hill, through the orchard, over the old-fashioned stile, across the corner of an 80-acre pasture and join Mona at the piano in her sitting room.

Like Mrs. Tracy, she had three decades of popular music dating back from before World War I through the latest sheet music. I would stand behind her and sing all the favorites as she played them. At times, we would end up playing and singing everything available.

Who, other than such an antique pop-tune geek, would remember World War II heroes such as Collin Kelly? Collin Kelly was an aviator whose plane received a direct hit from the guns on a Japanese battleship. As he came down, Kelly flew his plane directly into the smoke stack of that battleship and sunk it. Sometimes Mona's brother, Dale, a self-styled fiddler, would join in with his violin as we played and sang.

Preparatory to all of the above singing was music class in that one-room New Castle schoolhouse. We learned prescribed rural school vocal numbers our teacher played on an old crank-up Victrola. *Camp Town Races, Old Dog Tray,* and *Come, 'Tis a Rare Crystal Day* were not selections Ms. Boardman might have chosen, but they did whet my appetite for group singing, and later, formal choral groups.

Ms. Boardman's invitation first led to my singing in the "boys' chorus," then taking voice lessons and finally in my junior and senior high school years, singing in state contests with bass solos, boys' quartet, mixed quartet and madrigal, as well as boys' and mixed choruses.

An invitation by a wonderful music teacher led to my forming a male quartet my first year of college and singing together throughout four great years of college. It generated enough experience and confidence in my musical skills to form a dormitory chorus my sophomore year of college, win the University Sing three years running and retire a trophy for the Quadrangle Dormitory.

That one invitation by Ms. Boardman led to the joy of singing in the Iowa University Choir, and from there being invited to sing in the Chamber Singers Choir, a smaller select choir that sang modern creations. One of the joys of the large choir was to sing under the baton of such greats as Demetri Metropolis, who paid the University an annual visit as a personal friend of the orchestra director, Professor James Dixon.

Music has been a delicious and wonderfully important part of my life. This delectable serving of life's musical concoc-

Popular quartet at SUI — Fred at right (other individuals not identified).

Fred directing Quadrangle male chorus after winning the University sing.

tions came into my life because of a kind, gentle and persuasive invitation by a wonderful educator and musician, Ms. Eunice Boardman. (I'll sing a few bars to that!)

These invitations afforded me comfort and ease in public speaking and a significant outlet for both enjoyment and gentle expression throughout my career. I believe skills developed in the humanities lend invaluable assistance and grounding in ones professional experience. This would support the traditional requirement of the better part of a degree in basic sciences and the humanities before launching off into the medical profession.

■ CHAPTER 9 ■

The Art of Matching Desire with Reality

A SPECIAL HUMAN being progressed across the University of Iowa campus in lunging movements, up and down, extremities flailing, a Canadian crutch an awkward extension of his right arm; sometimes pointing toward the sky and other times a balancing ballast. As he moved, his facial contortions were symptomatic of his affliction — the heavy handicap of cerebral palsy.

Etched in my memory of campus life is one scene that I will never forget. At the center of the University campus is the Pentagon, remnants of the first capitol of Iowa. At the center of this two-square-block complex is "Old Gold," the first Capitol building of the state. At each of the four corners of this complex are previous government buildings — including one for the House, Senate and for the Treasury. Sidewalks surrounded the outer perimeter of the complex. From the midpoint of each side of the square a sidewalk runs directly to "Old Gold." Near the building itself, a walk surrounds the Capitol building. Diagonal walks connected the other administrative buildings with "Old Gold."

Early one winter morning the sidewalks on campus were partially covered with alternating areas of packed snow and sheets of ice created by snow melting the day before and refrozen that night. Scattered among the areas of treachery, dry sidewalk poked through where the sun had completed its task of melting the snow.

This particular morning, I was hurriedly walking from the

east side of the campus to one of the work assignments that sustained me financially. As I crossed campus from east to west, I walked around the south side of the Capitol building. Immediately in this anthill of bustling students scurrying along each of the many sidewalks, I identified David's right arm and Canadian crutch flailing desperately in the air. Students were passing on both sides and in opposite directions without pausing, apparently oblivious to David's plight.

As I came closer, I realized David was standing on a smooth patch of treacherous ice, frightened to death that he would fall and further embarrass himself while not having figured out how he could safely escape the danger. I greeted David, took his arm and assisted him off the ice in the direction from which I had come. Once safely on his way, I joined the anthill of students hurrying to their respective destinations.

Living on campus with David Rife provided numerous opportunities to observe him in various settings. This allowed me to see beyond his perpetual-motion torso, which was merely the surface of this man.

Academically, David was the epitome of intelligence, at the top of the heap among those sharing the campus at the University of Iowa. Beyond his keen wit and basic intelligence, he enjoyed a sense of humor, appreciation of community concerns and an understanding of international social needs. David presented with external confusion and speech impairment while internally was a highly organized individual with intellectual abilities that far outclassed our own.

On one occasion Jeanne, an attractive nursing student in our circle of friends, invited David to accompany her to a school function. On the surface this was a neat and thoughtful act. Introspectively, it gave him false hope that he might move into a normal dating relationship.

Encouraged by one encounter, David initiated an effort to date her again. Realizing this could become embarrassing for her, she declined. She was seriously interested in a young man who was not on campus and did not want to promote false hopes for David. Those of us in that circle of friends saw the disappointment David was experiencing. I am not aware of other dating efforts by Dave during our school years. Using his wisdom to overcome his desires, I am confident that he realized the gulf between his physical handicap and his intellectual and emotional ability.

We must each assess our personal environment, realistically matching clay and spirit, then becoming all that our human organism will allow. David could possibly become a world-class research expert in medicine. However, becoming a specialist in a field requiring delicate dexterity was "not in the cards."

▪ CHAPTER 10 ▪

The Art of Discipline

SPRING WAS AROUND the corner in 1956. Graduation from college was only a few months away, and I knew the Jackson County Draft Board would soon be breathing down this Class 1-A able-bodied young man's neck. I elected to contact the draft board to assess my status. I found that I was number 12 in line to be drafted.

It appeared "my number would be up" about the time of graduation. Being somewhat independent, I wanted to have some control over my destiny. I learned that if I enlisted, I would have the designation of Regular Army (RA) rather than a "draftee" (US); there were other benefits as well.

I learned that if I enlisted before I was drafted, the University would give me my standing grade without taking final exams. With everything else going on in preparation for entering the military service, it would be a relief not to worry about exams. Plus, if I wanted to extend my required period of duty by one year, I could choose available assignments overseas.

One option was a package which included six months of

Fred graduating in absentia.

57

Marge at graduation from SUI.

intensive basic training and then a tour in Germany. Having grown up with very little means, I figured that ever going "overseas" for me was not a likelihood. The guaranteed opportunity to visit my father's homeland and family seemed well worth

the additional year of service. I thought Marge, whom I married at the holiday break of this senior year, could join me there.

Visit to the farm before separation for the Army.

58

Basic Discipline

May 15, 1956, I was inducted into the United States Army at Fort Chaffee, Arkansas. This was a whole new experience. I had my first "crew cut" (the traditional military style). The haircut was a bit hideous but made less painful when wearing the olive drab cap we were issued, as well as the fact that everyone else had the same objectionable haircut.

I spent roughly two weeks at Fort Chaffee before receiving my orders for assignment. During this time we had exciting chores, such as kitchen police (KP), cleaning latrines and mopping the barracks. High on our list was cutting weeds with an "idiot stick." This was a straight stick with a "D"-shaped piece of metal at the distal end. The center portion of the curved part of the "D" was attached to the end of the stick. The flat part of the "D" was a double-edged blade which could be swung back and forth cutting a swath of grass or weeds in whichever direction it was swung.

Fred in uniform after induction.

"Military intelligence" was handed down by some of the troops who had arrived days to weeks ahead of us. This important information included such details as, "Don't ever volunteer for anything" and "Keep your name unknown as long as you can!" Reportedly, once one's name was known, that soldier's name was apt to be found on every detail list.

One's importance was verified one day when three of us lingered in the barracks (beneath the bunks) during the mass formation for detail assignments. We remained unnoticed and therefore not menaced while the remainder of the troops gained

*First military buddies
at Camp Chafffee, Ar-
kansas (individuals
not identified).*

expertise at swinging the "idiot sticks" for the balance of the day. Retrospectively, we would probably still be cleaning latrines if the non-commission officer had looked in the barracks that day.

When calls came for special talents, such as typing, I gave it a try. I purchased a typewriter while in college, learned what I knew from the guide book on my own and was never very proficient. Needless to say, I did not land a select assignment that would supersede the "idiot stick."

After a couple of weeks of "fun and games," my orders finally arrived and I was assigned to a heavy mortar company at Fort Ord, California, a post near Monterey, California, now closed. My first reward for being Regular Army then came to pass. The six or eight of us who were R.A. were flown commercially to Fort Ord. Other troops were transported by bus, train and military cargo planes.

Once in Fort Ord, we drew additional items beyond underclothing, olive drab fatigues, boots and billed cap for everyday wear. A khaki uniform with matching "cunt cap" and brown dress shoes were added. Included in the gear we drew from the quartermaster was an M-1 rifle with bayonet, gas mask, canteen, eating utensils, backpack and an entrenching tool (folding shovel).

Part of the processing included lining up for an appropriate series of inoculations for overseas travel. During this orientation period we began more formal detail duties while waiting for our first session of basic training to actually begin. "Detail" tasks included falling into line and policing the parade grounds every day. In the 1950s, smoking was popular in the United States. This was even more popular in the military services. The problem lay in the fact that everyone in the service above our rank of "private — E-1" (the lowest rank in the Army) felt that it was just fine to smoke a cigarette and discard the butt on the ground wherever the cigarette might be finished.

Each morning after the usual chores in the barracks and marching to and from breakfast, the whole company would "fall out" and line up across the parade field. We then walked from the side of the field away from the ocean toward the side of this huge field nearest the ocean. When we started, the morning fog was uniformly so thick we could not see from one side of the field to the other. Repeatedly, we would hear the sergeant shout, "Begin policing! I don't want to see anything but A-holes and elbows." Perhaps the only more common statement we heard from the sergeant was, "You ain't nothing but chow hounds."

The program I enlisted in was for the purpose of training "packet replacement platoons." One of the divisions in Germany was rotating back to the states. Our first three months in this assignment was concentrated on the bare Army basics. We had to learn how to care for our weapons. We learned how to totally dismantle an M-1 rifle and a carbine and put them back together, blindfolded. We learned to march in formation, qualify in riflery and study basic military theory.

During this time we pulled guard duty. There were several posts around the fort, but the most challenging was walking the sand dunes that overlooked the Pacific Ocean. We walked an assigned course back and forth throughout the entire shift. As we walked in either the dark, or sometimes moonlight, we could hear and often see the whitecaps as they broke on the shore. I could imagine a Japanese sub coming into the harbor, upping its periscope and watching me on guard duty.

An interesting aside was the fact that Gary Crosby, Bing's son, was assigned to our unit. However, he was usually away at some USO event at the Officers' Club locally, or as far away as Los Angeles. Other than the paper trail, it was my impression that his major activity was in Special Services.

Tab Hunter, an up-and-coming young movie star of that era, was making a "war movie" utilizing the troops in the unit housed in the building next to ours.

Each three-story building housed a company composed of three platoons. The diversity among the occupants was great. A limited number of us were college graduates. Most were just good old boys with no real ambition in life, other than to get their military service obligation behind them.

While at the fort, there were many lessons in discipline to be learned. In the learning process, we experienced a spectrum from outstanding examples to gross violations. Some particular examples have lingered in my memory throughout this half-century.

Jeff

One lad, I will call him Jeff, was a slight built, wiry young fellow who had a wife and five children. He was a compulsive gambler and always had a pair of dice in his pocket. He wanted to wager anything and everything he could get his hands on for a simple roll of the dice.

We were paid very little as "Private E-1s," and we had to share that meager amount with our spouse. My monthly pay at that time was $117. Ninety dollars of this went to my wife directly in the form of a allotment check. This left $27 per month for me to use for toothpaste, seats to a very inexpensive movie, on post and so forth. Since I had very little needs outside of that which was furnished — food, clothing and housing — I shared most of my $27 with my wife, Marge.

Jeff still stands out in my mind because I recall him receiving his check, immediately returning to the platoon area and addressing all the fellows who liked to gamble with a curt offer, "Roll you for your check." With every affirming nod, he would roll the dice against the barracks wall. When he lost the bet, he would turn over the entire portion of his month's pay to his fellow recruit, who had a smaller family with lesser needs than his own.

Tank

"Tank" was the nickname we gave to a fellow who most certainly weighed between 300 and 400 pounds. The quartermaster did not have uniforms large enough to fit him. The seamstress on post modified his trousers by sewing in additional panels of material on both sides. We all cheered when near the end of the first three months of basic training Tank was able to get into the largest unaltered military uniform.

At the firing range, Tank assumed the prone position more like a beached whale than a rifleman. The majority of the time he missed the entire target. The target was lowered into the trench, score recorded by the troopers in the trench, and "Maggie's drawers" were raised and waved when the target had been missed completely (a white flag on a broomstick symbolizing a total miss). For this effort, Tank acquired another nickname, "Bolo."

NCOs

Our NCOs were exceptionally disciplined soldiers. Our sergeant, the one who referred to us as "chow hounds," was an African-American fellow. He was meticulous in his dress. His fatigue uniform was starched to the Nth degree. The creases were so sharp they could cut bread. In order to keep them from being wrinkled, his wife would drive him to the barracks with him sitting crosswise in the back seat of their car with his legs outstretched. It was fashionable at that time to have the trouser legs neatly bloused above the boots. In order to make his uniform look pristine, he placed a four-inch circle of tin cut from a gallon can in each trouser leg. This held the trouser legs in a neat uniform circle bloused above his boots with the lower trouser legs tucked into his boots.

Our corporal was a Spanish-American gentleman who had spent nearly two years in and out of solitary confinement in a Korean prisoner of war camp. He had spent several months in a 3x3-foot bamboo cage out in the hot sun and rain where he was not able to stretch out full length. At the risk of being killed, he dismantled part of the cage and escaped in the night, finding his way back to the American lines. Needless to say, he served as an impressive role model.

Advanced Basic: Final Half

The final half of our six months' training in preparation for overseas duty was as an attachment to a heavy mortar company. During these three months we moved beyond the qualification with the M-1 rifle, carbine and 50-caliber machine gun. Our major training was in the use of the heavy mortar. In our first three months we also trained with live rifle ammunition on obstacle courses where we learned to crawl over fences, under barriers and around obstacles — continually prepared to fire live ammunition at targets that popped up across the course ahead of us. It was impressed on us to keep our weapons "up and down range" at all times and to move forward in a straight line. To impress on us the dangers inherent in this exercise, before starting the process of "running the course," we were grouped around a bronze plaque at the entry of the course listing the names of the soldiers who had been killed accidentally by careless comrades.

In the second three-month segment, we learned the mechanism and idiosyncrasies of the mortar. We first learned to assemble, dismantle and rapidly move it to a new location. A typical hard day's work would include marching 10 miles to Camp Hunter's Liggett where we would immediately begin digging three-foot deep mortar pits, 12 feet in diameter. These were dug in dry, hardened clay that most closely resembled concrete. The only tool we had to accomplish this was the entrenching tool, a small shovel that folded upon itself and was strapped to our backpack.

After multiple practice runs with the mortar, we would fill the hole, pack up the mortar and march back to the fort. During the two-hour march back to the barracks on the hard-packed dirt road, seemingly covered with an inch or more of powder-like silt, a poison gas alert would be issued. We immediately stopped and put on our gas masks which, like our entrenching tools, were attached to our backpack. We then marched the remainder of the way back in the near 100-degree heat with the masks strapped to our faces. While training on the mortar, we trained further with small arms, 50-caliber machine guns and bazookas.

Eventually, we took the mortars out to a firing range. Here, smaller sleeve inserts were placed in the barrels of the mortars. This allowed us to fire smaller rounds and use smaller amounts of explosives while still achieving the objective of learning the skill of bracketing in the target and "firing for effect." The explosives came in a package with 10 charges per package. Depending on the location of our targets — wrecked automobile bodies placed throughout a wide open field — we generally placed two or three charges in the chamber.

One day we had firsthand experience in what could have been a military training catastrophe. Apparently, because of the tightness of the training areas available, classes of recruits were in didactic training on bleachers straight out (one range over) from our firing range. As our captain barked out the location of targets, each team calculated the appropriate number of charges needed, placed them in the chamber and prepared for the instruction to fire. Bracketing was done by noting whether the first round was long or short, aiming nearer or farther from the target, depending on the site of the first round exploded, then estimating the position of the target between the two rounds and making the appropriate corrections in charges and angle of the trajectory.

During this exercise, the captain observed the crew's accuracy through his binoculars. After firing for some time, the captain commented to his NCO that there apparently was someone firing on a distant range beyond the troops in the bleachers. After reflecting for a moment and recalling no other units were to be practicing that day, he screamed, "Cease-fire!" It suddenly became apparent to him that one of the mortar teams in our company was placing all 10 charges in the barrel and firing right over the heads of the troops in the bleachers.

We were firing live "H & E" rounds that were lesser than regular heavy mortar rounds. Nonetheless, should such a round strike the bleachers, it would very likely wound or kill numerous soldiers. It was easy to understand how, in the heat of war, multiple similar incidents can occur without benefit of warning plaques, as we saw on the rifle and mortar ranges.

Other less deadly threats were numerous and in the form of tarantula spiders and scorpions. The tarantulas peppered the dusty roads, and one could see where cars tracks would swing from the center of the road to a squashed spider and then back to the center. During one of our overnight outings beneath a "pup tent," I received a morning greeting from a scorpion sitting on my duffel bag when I started to open it and prepare for the day.

New Level of Discipline

During the second three-month basic training period, the captain, who was commissioned in the Reserve Officer Training Corps (ROTC) in college, came to me as a fellow college graduate. He shared his thought that I, having a college education, was too bright not to improve on my military rank. He suggested I apply for Officer Candidate School (OCS); he offered to write a recommendation for me.

About the midpoint of my six-months training, my wife and her mother drove our 1948 Chevrolet to Fort Ord. Marge found a room to rent with the wife and family of an Army captain who had received a hardship tour in the Far East. Her mother then returned to Iowa. This home happened to be located only a block or two from the Mission in Carmel. Marge thoroughly enjoyed daily short walks to Carmel Beach, and somehow during my weekend passes found a way to become pregnant.

With this new consideration, I realized that I could not continue the plan to go to Germany with the packet platoon. There would be no way I could transport her and a new baby to Europe and pay for her food and lodging off base. With a small baby, the chance of her

Marge and Fred with commission and awaiting first child.

finding work would be even more difficult.

Having considered all of these factors, I accepted the captain's offer, filled out the OCS application, and as the second session neared completion, I received orders to go to OCS at Fort Benning, Georgia.

■ CHAPTER 11 ■

The Art of Advanced Discipline

THE ACCEPTANCE TO OCS brought a new understanding of discipline. The concept that once one received a degree from college there was an automatic license for free thinking was soon dispelled.

En route from California to Georgia, I first had to take my newly pregnant wife to her parents' home in Moorhead, Iowa, and continue on to Columbus, Georgia by myself. After finding the post and registering at the battalion headquarters, I immediately became "nobody," referred to by my "TAC (Training and Command) Officer" as "Candidate Hahn."

My college vocabulary was quickly reduced to three phrases shouted in loud tones: "Yes, sir!" "No, sir!" and "No excuse, sir!" After being assigned a room in the barracks and acquiring a roommate, Ed Habeck, to share six months of hazing, I was off to learn this new level of discipline.

Preliminary to the school, I was promoted to E-5. The intent of the training program was to convert this company of Non-Commissioned Officers (noncoms) into "Officers and Gentlemen" capable of leading troops into combat. The class was composed of a wide variety of candidates ranging from persons like myself, who had little military experience, to seasoned non-commissioned officers who had suffered the rigors of terrible combat.

Ed came from a background of a ski troop instructor in the Alps. He was short, stocky and hard as nails. His legs were like pistons, and he could do squat jumps from morning till night.

My next best friend was Jim Hoeh. His most recent wartime experience had been in Korea where he was the first sergeant in a parachute machine gun company. His unit was dropped on a hill right on the frontlines now famous for the number of casualties. With coaxing, he related the story of his lieutenant being killed shortly after entering combat. It was widely rumored that the "half-life" of a second lieutenant in battle was two and one-half minutes. Being the ranking NCO, Jim assumed command of the company. Soon, hand-to-hand combat ensued. He had to call in artillery fire right on top of his location. Jim was one of only a handful of men from his entire company who survived the battle. He was the epitome of discipline and dedication.

Throughout this six-month training period — designed to turn us into what was commonly referred to as "Six-month Wonders"— we had daily instructional courses covering everything from military organization to the idiosyncrasies of land mines. Candidates rotated for one week in each of the positions from private to captain in a classic infantry company. In each role, the candidate assumed all of the responsibilities of the rank, not only in formation, but in the activities of the day.

Physical activities included the "daily dozen" exercises, as well as running on the track, marching, and later on difficult obstacle and infiltration courses (the best-known being the "airborne course").

We learned how to handle troops marching in formation both as related to the company itself and in battalion formations on parade grounds. In this area, I was fortunate enough to be selected for the company's "crack" drill team that competed with all other companies in the training battalion. Our company was blessed with a candidate who had been the Sergeant of the Guard at Arlington Cemetery. He taught us everything from "monkey drills" to the "Queen Anne Salute" and

Fred's drill team in OCS (Fred is the second person behind drill team leader).

made it possible for us to quite handily win the Battalion Drill Teams competition.

Throughout our training, discipline was learned through what we knew in college as "hazing." The beds were made in the morning such that a quarter would bounce on striking the bed from a height of three feet. The drawers had every item folded neatly and placed in a prescribed manner. The laundry bag was tied in a prescribed manner at the foot of the bed. All items in the room were uniform throughout the company and similarly placed in the appropriate position. The light fixtures in rooms were polished with Brasso to the brilliance of a mirror, as were our belt buckles. Our two pairs of boots were always "spit-shined" daily, worn on alternate days, with the shoelaces placed so that the strings were beneath the holes on the bottom two eyelets on one pair of shoes and over the eyelets on the opposite pair. The "over/under" rule of having the laces appropriate for that prescribed day led to demerits if one was out of sync. The two pairs of boots were both required to have the same reflective shine even if they had been in wet mud the entire day before.

Before leaving the room each morning, the tile floors were buffed with a large buffer with a towel beneath it so they would "stand as tall" (shine) as our buckles, shoes and light fixtures.

When we came in tired after a hard day in the field, a fresh TAC Officer would meet us, take off to the track and run us until we were ready to drop. We then went to our barracks. In the rooms we would find our bed torn up, all our drawers emptied on the bed and floor and our laundry bag untied and emptied on the floor. In the hall there would be a list of all the hypothetical shortcomings in the room; the bristles of the toothbrush pointed the wrong way, the knot on the laundry bag incorrect, and on and on. For each manufactured errant deed, demerits were assigned. Above a certain level, privileges were taken away. For example, one might have to stay in his room and not go to the day room.

At "14" weeks, the candidates who had not been "washed out" (kicked out) in weekly review panels "turned blue." This meant that a light blue felt stripe was placed on the epaulet of our uniforms, and it was beginning to look like we might make it.

After turning blue, and if our total number of demerits was low enough, there was the possibility of a few hours pass on weekends. The wives of the married men were for the first time allowed to acquire their own housing and be available to see their mates in those few hours.

Early on in these last weeks, one would have the privilege of visiting his spouse in the day room. Sometimes that privilege would be only an hour; other times, not at all. We had no way to communicate our degree of freedom to our spouses. Marge and other spouses would not uncommonly come to the day room, wait all evening and not get to see us at all.

The last night before "turning blue," the lights in the barracks came on at 2 a.m. We were directed to be ready to fall

Rare opportunity to be with spouses.

into formation in 20 minutes. The prescribed uniform was long underwear under training shorts, boots with no socks, a metal helmet with no liner, and our top dresser drawer with all its contents under our right arm. On the command to "fall in," we rushed out into the dark and fell into company formation. Here we were instructed to go through various positions from "attention" to "parade rest" to "run in place."

One can imagine the scene with helmets banging up and down on our heads and the drawers being unmercifully jumbled. This was our last major lesson in learning to be humble and obedient before moving on toward thoughts of becoming a true leader.

Once commissioned a second lieutenant, I received a requested transfer to the Army Medical Service Corps (AMSC) in San Antonio where I served the final two years of my military career, where both of my daughters were born and from where I applied for and was accepted into medical school at the University of Iowa.

My requested transfer to AMSC was received with some

ribbing, but quickly countered by a reminder that I had the best score in the entire company on the rifle range.

I feel that my military experience, and particularly OCS, gave me a healthy respect for authority at all levels, whether that be rank, age or academic prowess.

I learned that the discipline of following a prescribed set of directions or course of actions is generally a trustworthy and safe route to a goal.

An officer and a gentleman.

Although those of us who experienced a military obligation often spoke of "the right way, the wrong way and the Army way," the discipline of a repeated, tested and improved course of action is generally a dependable approach. Here, the keyword is "discipline."

CHAPTER 12

The Art of Enthusiasm

WHEN I MARRIED Marge, I married a beekeeper's daughter. I also had an unsolicited opportunity to learn a whole new cultural medium. St. Augustine is credited with comparing the world to a book. "If a person does not travel to countries other than his own," he said, "that person has read but a single chapter."

Having grown up on a farm, I am well acquainted with hard physical labor. Working in a bee business (apiary) was a new chapter in my book of "hard labor." Such was my lot during the summer breaks of my first and second years of medical school.

Marge's father, Walter Weldon, worked as a caddie at a golf course in Berkeley, California, during the Great Depression of 1929. He later drove lumber trucks over the Rocky Mountains and sought other challenging jobs to escape the consequences of the depression on his small family.

In 1939, he and his wife moved to Jeannette's childhood home in Nebraska. One year later, he followed his eldest brother, Roy, to Iowa. Roy had elected to earn a living in the bee business. Walter initially rented a home in the country near Moorhead and worked out of this rented rural home setting. Things were really tough then. He and Jeannette had only enough money for gas and food for three-year-old Marge and one-and-a-half-year-old brother, Lloyd. They all slept in the car, and Walter and Jeannette ate nothing on the trip back.

As his apiary business grew, he bought a home in

Moorhead. When he found the honey business was still better in Colone, South Dakota, they began setting up work in a warehouse. During the summer months he and Jeannette lived in a tiny two-bedroom home with limited improvements (bare bulb electricity, cold water from the faucet, a sink with the luxury of a drain, and the classic "two-holer" down the 50-foot path from the kitchen door.

Now, 20 years later, hard work had led to a thriving bee business. During the summers following the three years in the service and after the first year of medical school, Marge and I were available laborers. We certainly needed work and sustenance.

Our family of four occupied one bedroom of the Weldon's primitive "summer home." The larger room served as dining

Lessons from the bee community.

room, family room and sitting room. It was shared by all in the extended family.

Bathing was necessarily done in non-meal serving periods when the curtain could be pulled between the kitchen (doubling as the bath) and the larger common area. Warm water heated on the stove was right at our elbows. For a country boy like, me it was as Yogi Berra said, "Déjà vu all over again."

The work was comparable to the intense hard work one experiences on a farm, save for the necessarily miserable nuisance of working in the hot summer months with leather gloves, a hat with a bee veil over one's head and trouser legs tucked into high-top work shoes.

However, hard labor has its lighter moments. Along the way, I learned cute little things, such as why bees buzz: "You'd buzz, too, if someone took your honey and necked her," and "The bee's stinger is only two millimeters long; the rest is enthusiasm!"

It was interesting to find that only one "Queen" was allowed in each hive. Queen bees are groomed by worker bees feeding the larva special food called royal jelly. Fed thusly, a few of the thousands of eggs laid each day by the Queen bees are nurtured into larger female bees, two to three times the size of a regular female worker bee.

When the larvae hatch, the first Queen to hatch stings all the remaining queen larvae, and she then takes over the colony of bees. The old queen, unable to tolerate two female rulers in the same house (hive) leaves, along with a goodly portion of the bees who are loyal to her. This departure of the old Queen with a portion of the colony weakens the number remaining for a time until the new Queen lays and hatches enough eggs to replenish the hive.

This is particularly undesirable during the height of the honey-producing season as it is as if half of one's labor force (from that hive) quits or leaves. Therefore, the beekeeper watches the hives carefully and destroys the Queen bee larva cells even before the first ones hatch.

There are those who isolate each new Queen Bee cell and produce Queens for beekeepers who wish to expand their number of hives. The male bees, drones, are reputed to be lazy. They seemingly sit gleefully at home (in the hive) while the female (worker) bees are flying several miles to collect nectar and pollen.

The worker bees literally beat their wings to pieces flying back and forth. They truly fall in the line of duty while the drones sit safely in the hive with their wings in perpetual motion. In fact, they are a living ventilation system that dries and cures the nectar into thickened honey, ready for each cell to be capped.

Perhaps, not unlike Marge's parents' experience in the Depression, we were thankful for a source of a small income, maintenance of the family, and a warm and loving family situation. Here, I was able to observe the same discipline of hard labor and the squeaky- clean work ethic common to both Walter and my father.

The second summer was encumbered by Marge's being in a short-legged cast following our freshman year car wreck and her initial ankle fracture repair. She had just reached the stage of a walking cast as this summer began. This was an added challenge in her caring for the children, helping her mother and, to some degree, helping with the warehouse chores. Marge's first cousin, Terry, and his wife, Shirley, and family worked for Walter and Jeannette as their primary hired help at that time. Although Terry was experienced in bee work, I was experienced in hard farm work. With each of us being furiously competitive, we had summers of constantly trying to outdo each other.

We worked long hours, usually extended in the warehouse

after a full day's work in the bee yards. Working together, we had goals of beating all the records of single-day's honey extraction that Walter recorded with previous employees (or with him and Jeannette). For many years, Jeannette worked equally as hard as Walt.

It was not uncommon to get in from the field at 6 p.m., eat the great farm-style supper the women prepared, and then return to the warehouse until 10 or 11 p.m. extracting honey and getting the empty supers (boxes open at the top and bottom which held the frames of wax) ready to place back on the truck and take to the yards the next day.

Through the consistency, discipline and energy exhibited by every bee in each colony, we found they could produce up to 200 pounds of clear sweet honey in each hive every summer.

As I experienced the harmony and enthusiasm of these miniature societies and then enjoyed the fruits of their labor, there has to "bee" a lesson here for those of us who practice in our medical communities.

Perhaps part of that lesson was, "A bee's stinger is only 2 mm long; the rest is enthusiasm."

CHAPTER 13

The Art of Redundancy

ONCE THE TWO grueling years of intense didactic medical courses were completed, the opportunity came for the clinical application of what we had learned.

If there ever was such a thing as safety in repetition, the university clinical medical training of the 1960s should have been safe. In essence, patients were protected by a six-tiered system.

When a hospital patient was admitted, temperature, pulse, respiration, blood pressure, weight, medicines and allergies were recorded by a nurse or an orderly. Each patient was provided the classic "semi private" gown with "southern exposure."

The First Tier

When one of the five medical students assigned to the ward was alerted to a new admission, he/she (at this point only five percent of the class was female) quickly set the first tier in progress. With a pad of clinical notepaper in hand, he struck out for the patients cubicle — made private only by a series of curtains that hung from a track on the ceiling surrounding the bed.

Patients were seen in a regular rotation by the students. The medical student methodically paged item by item through a pocket-size physical diagnosis manual asking detailed questions and recording equally detailed responses. The responses were supposed to be written in legible longhand (some clinical instructors required printed or typed histories and physicals, known as "H&Ps").

This series of questions included the patient's chief complaint (CC); a chronology of the present illness (PI); a past history (PH) of allergies, medicines used, previous surgeries, previous injuries and significant illnesses; a history of family illnesses (FH) with detailed findings in the nearest of kin; a review of the major body systems (ROS) and a social history (SH) including the use of tobacco, alcohol and drugs, as well as any important interpersonal relationships.

When this laborious mental exercise was completed, an equally detailed physical examination (PE) began. Not being so verbose as to detail this examination, let it be said that it included everything from an ophthalmascopic exam of the internal eye at one end, to a pelvic and rectal exam at the other.

Once this H&P was finished, a list of suspected clinical diagnoses was recorded, a plan for laboratory documentation of these entities was outlined and a course of clinical management proposed. This concluded the first tier of what — to the patient — often became a lengthy and tiring chain of events.

Recently I was privileged to review a medical record of a patient who was suing a physician for a postoperative complaint. The patient claimed the symptoms were a consequence of recent surgery. However, the student's clearly written history documented the complaint on admission and as a preoperative, preexisting complaint. This detailed documentation substantiated the physician's position and the suit was dropped.

The Second Tier

The second tier evaluation was completed by what in the 1960s was termed the "rotating intern." This physician spent a predetermined amount of time on both a male and a female medical and surgical ward, a stint in obstetrics and gynecology, a stint in pediatrics, and usually a month on the emergency room service. Generally, there were two or three months left to spend in elective areas the intern thought would be helpful in general practice, or in an area that pointed toward a residency in a specified specialty.

At the university, medicine and surgery wards were served by two rotating interns. Each intern was responsible for half of the ward. Needless to say, the intern could not spend as much time with the patient as the student. The same basic questions were asked, in abbreviated form, and only the positive findings and pertinent negative findings were recorded. The intern had both the benefit and responsibility of reviewing the student's detailed H&P, which filled in some of the less important minutia. After the intern's work-up, he or she outlined the clinical work-up or simply approved that already detailed by the student, thus ending the second tier of the medical evaluation.

The Third Tier

The third tier was the responsibility of a first-year resident. He/she was responsible for the entire ward of 25 to 30 acutely ill patients.

These more abbreviated evaluations pointed toward the crux of the patient's reason for admission. The resident's previous years of the repetitive steps outlined above, plus an expanded pool of experience and didactic training, contributed to the ability to be concise. The resident further fine-tuned the necessary laboratory requests and made appropriate adjustments to the intern's treatment plan.

The first two tiers were a reinforcement of the resident's assessment and simultaneously proved instructive for the intern and medical student assigned to the patient.

The Fourth Tier

The chief resident accomplished the fourth tier of the system. This senior resident had completed the requirements of a junior resident: one year on the wards and a second year in the specialty clinics. In the clinic setting he/she gained knowledge in specialty and subspecialty areas such as allergy, hematology, endocrinology, gastroenterology, cardiology, urology, neurology and infectious disease.

The chief resident's role was primarily directed at being available at any time to assist the resident-in-charge with care of the more acutely ill patients.

Intensive care units in general, and specialty intensive care units in particular, were not common in university hospital settings in the 1960s. Where these units were available, they were usually a four to six bed ward reserved for the most seriously ill or complicated cases on each of the medical or surgical floors. The chief resident was the physician-in-charge. She/he drew interesting and instructive cases usually from the smaller ward and presented the clinical material (case studies) for the weekly clinical pathologic conferences (CPCs), which were attended by medical students, interns, residents and staff.

The Fifth Tier

The fifth tier was conducted by the staff clinician. The staff doctor assigned to the ward made regularly scheduled rounds three times a week on the medical wards. Depending on the "attending's" individual sense of responsibility and the time available from private and research assignments, he/she was on call in a rotation with the other doctors staffing the medicine (or surgery) wards. They generally were not bothered unless a true emergency existed.

During rounds, the staff clinician led the discussion on each case, enlarged on the nature of the illnesses represented in the patients and reviewed the appropriateness of each patient's care (this position deserves a number of chapters in itself).

The Sixth Tier

The final tier was, in reality, two in one. This tier consisted, first, of the clinical sub-specialists from the various specialties enumerated in the review of systems as outlined by the medical student. Accompanying the professor was an entourage of second-year residents rotating through the clinics and any senior residents specializing in the specialty. This tier was available to discuss problem cases in the particular specialty area(s) and to consult on the specific case(s).

From this institutional milieu as a backdrop, I hope to share some insightful treasures which life in the medical profession provided me through the art of medicine.

■ CHAPTER 14 ■

The Art of Speed Bumps

THE PROVISION OF living quarters for married college students has likely been a problem as long as there have been married students. At The State University of Iowa in the early 1960s, "Quonset hut" apartments, large old homes made into apartments and trailer parks were the most common locations available for young, financially challenged married students.

The first time I remember seeing "speed bumps" was in the trailer park near North Dubuque Street in Iowa City in the early 1960s. Some of our medical student classmates lived there. At that time, speed bumps seemed to be a uniquely new, yet practical solution to protect the herd of small children roaming the park with the abandon of an open range.

Today, speed bumps have become commonplace in shopping centers, gated communities and, in fact, are so commonplace they have come to mean any type of deterrent to one's frenetic race through life.

Our budding family's course down the highway to a medical degree encountered numerous sets of speed bumps. The first major field of speed bumps appeared in the spring of our first year of medical school at Iowa City. Marge's mother, Jeannette, had agreed to take our two girls to Moorhead in western Iowa for the weekend while we traveled to Maquoketa in eastern Iowa for the wedding of a distant cousin, who lived in the same community and had attended elementary school in a class just behind me at New Castle.

After Marge and I attended church with my parents, I drove

the family car from our church in the tiny village of Fulton toward Maquoketa, some six miles away. We intended to eat in our small county seat town and then attend the wedding there in town.

It was a blustery dark spring day with snow showers; yet the temperature was warm enough to prevent any accumulation. As we approached the 45 mph zone at Hurstville, two miles north of Maquoketa, a station wagon with a couple of adults and a half-dozen children slowed to turn off the road to the right from their oncoming direction. A second car with a priest and his driver came right behind them, slowing to accommodate for the first auto's slowing speed prior to turning. This all occurred without our particular notice as we visited joyfully about all that was taking place in both our parents' lives and our own.

Suddenly, behind the first two cars, a one-and-a-half-ton milk truck closed in on the other cars without slowing. The truck struck the second car in the rear, driving it into the turning station wagon. It then suddenly bounced out into our lane, following the driver's last-minute effort to miss the rear of the second vehicle.

This all occurred in just a couple of car lengths in front of us. In an effort to miss the truck, I reacted with one desperate turn of my steering wheel to the right. Only the outer right half of our car cleared the truck. With the impact of the left front of my parents' 1955 Chevrolet sedan against the left front of the truck, there was a stunning thud which caused one's memory to pause.

Our car's rear end lifted from the highway with the crash, swung around perpendicular to the truck and then settled back on the edge of the highway as both vehicles came to a stop. We learned later, the day before the accident, the truck had some work done on the brakes that were faulty, and this caused complete brake failure when the driver forcefully applied them.

In my instantaneous preparation for the crash, I braced my hands and arms against the steering wheel. With the impact, each side of the steering wheel was wrapped down around the steering column. The effort was unsuccessful in preventing the cone-shaped center of the wheel from striking me squarely in the sternum (breast bone). This was before seat belts.

After a momentary lapse of awareness, I looked across the front seat to my right. Marge, in the middle, was slouched down, but was conscious. She had braced her left foot on the raised central drive shaft column. The impact drove the distal long bones of her left leg over her ankle joint, creating a severe trimaleolar fracture/impaction. At the same time, her body was thrown forward. Her forehead struck the rearview mirror, breaking it off and, in turn, broke the mid-portion of the windshield. Her alertness masked the seriousness of her injuries.

Next to Marge, my sister Berta was thrown like a free missile, forehead first, into the windshield, which shattered into hundreds of small pieces. The fragments of glass placed a nearly equal number of check-like cuts in her forehead, collectively yielding a bloody gore. She was unconscious and having trouble maintaining an airway (my parents were convinced she had "swallowed her tongue"). I'll never forget my fleeting thought: "Well, Mom and Dad still have two living children." (I don't believe I ever shared this with Berta.)

My parents were thrown forward against the back of the front seat. My mother received the most severe back-seat injuries, deep triangular lacerations in her shin areas, tearing through skin and muscle right down to bone.

The surge of "fright and flight" allowed me to spring out of my side of the car, run around to the opposite side, use what medical knowledge I had to establish Berta's airway and then lift her from the front seat and carry her to one of the cars stopped behind us. We then hurried off to the Maquoketa Community Hospital, without modern considerations for possible cervical injuries.

Other carloads of church people who arrived with the same initial lunch/wedding plans, jumped out of their cars and assisted Marge and my parents. Again, at that time I didn't realize the severity of Marge's injuries, which through the years have proven to be by far the most severe.

On the way to the hospital, Berta began to regain consciousness. She was lying across the back seat of the assisting auto with her head on my lap. Only then did I begin to realize that my parents would likely still have three living children.

Dr. Broman, who had cared for us through our young adult years, came to the hospital this Sunday to care for our needs. By the time we arrived in the emergency room for evaluation, my chest became so painful I could hardly move. That night, because of my chest pain, I spent all of 45 minutes trying to turn from my back to my stomach, only to find it even more uncomfortable, and then spent an equal length of time returning to my back.

Marge was in a great deal of pain, despite her leg and ankle being stabilized with a cast. In a couple of days, we were all out of the hospital, except Marge. At four days post injury, the doctors believed she could travel by car to the University Hospitals in Iowa City.

In the following weeks, my sister's lacerations healed without incident, save for pieces of glass that worked out of her forehead for months. Berta did fine for years, but in her 40s developed an episode of ascending neuropathy (feeling of pins and needles, like a waking limb) from her toes to her saddle area. This passed, only to be followed by a syncopal/convulsive episode that on an MRI evaluation appeared to be related to scar tissue in the frontal compartment of her brain, apparently from the auto accident years earlier.

My parents suffered the arthritides typical of injuries sustained in adult life, but otherwise fared pretty well.

Marge was another story. We proceeded directly to the University of Iowa Hospitals for definitive surgery on her ankle. When the cast was removed, it was found that she had an area of pressure necrosis on the dorsum of her foot. The swelling had rendered the cast too tight and left a severe pressure sore — one reason for her seeming excessive pain. The ankle specialist, Dr. Bonfiglio, operated on her ankle using a number of screws to put it back together. He warned her, "In the future the joint will likely become so painful that you will have to have this ankle fused." This one large "speed bump" generated second and third generation bumps.

More Bumps

Marge's mother was kind enough to keep our two girls at her home in Moorhead where we were to rendezvous during Easter vacation had the accident not occurred. Marge's condition led to a lengthy separation from the girls during this most difficult of times. Marge had been teaching, and her income was lost.

The liability insurance carried by the one-man auto shop that had worked on the truck's brakes was limited and proved to be only enough to cover those less seriously injured, plus Marge's initial medical expenses. The mechanic was himself a handicapped person with a large family and limited means. Both we and our lawyer felt it best not to push beyond the limits of his insurance coverage due to his pre-existing hardships.

The largest bump was the final medical school exams. I was no more than an average medical student. These circumstances allowed me to do only well enough on final exams to be offered the opportunity to extend my training one additional year (this we elected to do only after serious deliberation).

Still More Bumps

There was a bevy of smaller speed bumps. Some are now laughable, others still painful. Back in Iowa City, our friendly insurance man came by the house to talk to Marge while she was still in a full-leg (foot to thigh) cast following her initial ankle reconstruction. He was thoughtful and kind. He helped her to the sofa and then placed her crutches across the room against the wall while they talked. When he got up to leave, both he and Marge forgot the location of the crutches as he offered to leave unassisted. After he was gone, she realized she could not get up from the sofa or walk without them. The insurance man's visit was right after lunch, and she was most anxious to see me when I came home from medical school. After I handed her the crutches, she hurried up the stairs to our second floor (and only) bathroom in our two-level duplex.

One heart-rending note: Mrs. Weldon brought Debbie (then three) and Kathy (two) back home three months after the accident. When Marge's mother brought them into the house, they just stood looking at us with puzzled expressions which said,

Marge with initial cast after the ankle repair.

"Who are these people?" (A gut-wrenching feeling we'll never forget.)

Marge's cast was shortened that summer to a lower leg cast, and finally a rubber walker was placed on the sole to allow her to walk. That summer I worked for her parents in their honey bee business in Colone, South Dakota.

Marge's extended complications did not end with medical school. Five years

Graduation to a brace assist in motherhood.

later, in December of our rotating internship year at Kansas City General Hospital, we celebrated our ninth wedding anniversary. We had a delightful dinner at the Plaza III Restaurant. This was a rare luxury for our fragile budget.

The next day, while I was serving on one of my busiest rotations at old Children's Mercy Hospital (at the time still on Independence Avenue in Kansas City, Missouri), I received a call from my intern classmate's wife, Arlidene Nelson, who lived in the duplex across the street from us in Independence. She told me Marge had been out cracking nuts on the back steps in preparation for making Christmas candy. She had a sudden excruciating headache, was barely able to get back into the house to lie down and sent our preschool-age daughter, Kathy, to get Arlidene. It was suspected that she had another of the migraine headaches which she had experienced regularly since the auto wreck in medical school. Arlidene loaded Marge, who was nauseated and vomiting, into her car and took her to our friend and Marge's gynecologist's office. It was suspected that she just had another migraine. She was given a shot of Demerol and allowed to return home. Arlidene kept in touch with me by phone to keep me posted on her progress.

Even then, Children's Mercy Hospital was a recognized care center for critically ill children. Both General Hospital and Children's Mercy were at that juncture "interns hospitals." Interns were the major part of the professional workforce with only a few residents and permanent staff members. While my conscience told me I should be home with Marge, I felt a compelling need to care for the desperately ill children who were my wards.

Around 6 p.m. I was finally able to break away to go home. There, I found Marge more ill than I ever imagined. Her excruciating headache persisted and was associated with visual symptoms. I called Dr. Fouts, our personal friend and internist. Dallas, a fine physician of the old school, came directly from his office to our duplex, confirmed a cranial nerve deficit (diplopia) and suggested a spinal tap.

Marge was taken to the Independence Sanitarium and Hospital by ambulance, where I assisted Dallas in doing the spinal tap. The tap was grossly bloody. It became clear that Marge was experiencing a cerebral hemorrhage. Dr. William Wu, a respected neurosurgeon, was consulted. He carried out a cerebral arteriogram via a carotid artery puncture, which was routine at that time. This was done without the modern convenience of a rapid cossette changer. The verbal "squirt-shoot" technique of demonstrating the arterial and venous phases of the circulation showed some blurring in an area deep in the skull base referred to as the "siphon area."

Without a specific aneurysm or lesion to be addressed surgically, Dr. Wu elected to treat her conservatively with sedation and strict bed rest. Retrospectively, it was suspected that the bleed may have been a late consequence from the auto accident five years earlier. Following the accident, Marge continually complained of a sensation in the mid-brow area that she described as a bee buzzing in her head. This may well have been an arterio-venous malformation.

Marge's mother again picked up the slack, coming to our home and caring for the whole family while Marge recuperated. She kindly served as mother, nurse, grandmother, cook and housekeeper. Thankfully, Marge did return to her pre-bleed status. However, as we continued to move about in our training programs, we routinely signed in with a local neurologist soon after our arrival and had him available for any further "what ifs."

Bump Later On

Following the four years of medical school, a year of internship in Kansas City, a year of internal medicine at the University of Iowa, and a career change taking us to an Otolaryngology (ENT) residency at Mayo Clinic, Marge did indeed experience the predicted progression of arthritis in her left ankle. Seven years after her initial repair, she could walk only a few blocks and stand for a short time before she would suffer ankle pain. This took her to Dr. Mark Coventry, the head of the Orthopedic Department at Mayo Clinic, who recommended and carried out the ankle fusion predicted by Dr. Bonfiglio.

After once again progressing through a series of casts and braces, she experienced a tremendous reprieve from pain. In fact, we elected to take up golf together. We did so without lessons and on a newly constructed course at Simpson, Minnesota, some 20 miles from Rochester. On this course, in which the owner had illusions of golf grandeur, we searched for balls among the dandelions in the summer and piles of leaves on the rough greens and fairways in the fall. We struggled among the cows who still believed they possessed squatter's rights. The greens fee, nonetheless, was just "what the doctor (and budget) ordered!" Marge was blessed with her repair to the point she would at times walk 27 holes with little discomfort. She was so elated, she told Dr. Coventry on a post-op visit, "I'm so happy I could kiss you." In his rather dry proper English manner, he replied, "Don't restrain yourself."

Perhaps this is enough in the way of bumps for now. However, this cascade of our personal difficulties and setbacks taught me to be more attentive and sympathetic to those of my patients who suffered health problems with the associate heartache and hardships.

We struggled on through the next two years of clinical medical education without major incident.

I might add parenthetically that married students with children in diapers at the onset of medical school experience a degree of isolation and separation that did not seem to occur with students who studied together, shared old exams and "held hands" with their classmates.

■ CHAPTER 15 ■

The Art of Clinical Training

WHEN THE THIRD and fourth years of my extended four-year medical school program began, I was grateful the first two grueling years of basic science were finally behind me. I readily admit that the memorization and regurgitation of basic science information was neither my first love nor my forte.

But during my third-year clinical rotations, I began to recognize my gift of dealing with patients comfortably and to being at ease with them. The interchange during the taking of patient's medical and social history, followed by the "laying on of hands" in the physical examination, is a unique talent not necessarily bestowed on students with the greatest measurable academic ability.

It was during those next few years that I began to understand that to be a complete physician one must combine "principle and practice."

"Physical Diagnosis" was the only course offered during the sophomore year that pointed us toward the physical evaluation of a real patient in those clinical years. Again, it consisted of the supervised practice of actually taking a complete and appropriate history: CC, PI, PH, FH, ROS and SH.

Following this exercise, patients who willingly consented to help with the medical education of the students underwent a physical examination as part of a small group class for medical students. They were discreetly disrobed in front of the professor and a small group of students and one or more members of the group physically examined them while the professor and others in the small group observed and critiqued those doing the exam.

A Bit Nervous

I particularly recall one of my classmates, who was also a married student with children. While I served my years in the military service following my Bachelor of Science degree, he attended veterinary school. He graduated very near the top of his "vet" class and was nearly as outstanding in medical school. I specifically recall a discussion among our classmates during a "brown bag" lunch break following an early physical diagnosis class. He was receiving more than his share of rhubarb.

Reportedly, Bob became very staccato in his speech, clumsy in his hand movements, turned a rather inappropriate crimson color and perspired profusely while demonstrating proper physical examination techniques on a relatively attractive woman in her mid-30. I'm sure it was from just such a stressful situation that the often-told medical school story arose about a similar young male medical student.

As the story goes, on this appointed day, the professor, his five medical students, the nursing instructor, an equivalent number of student nurses, the two interns on the ward and the internal medicine resident-in-charge were all making teaching rounds together. They gathered around the bed of an attractive, well-endowed 18-year-old woman with the known diagnosis of RHD (rheumatic heart disease) and the associated classical heart murmur emanating from her damaged mitral valve. The curtains were pulled around her bed to isolate her and this entourage from the rest of the ward.

The professor designated a young male medical student to be the first to examine the young woman's heart and describe her physical findings. Faithful to the principle that one must properly expose "the anatomy" in question to identify the disease, the professor turned the sheet down to her navel. He then loosened the strings at the neck of her semi-private gown and similarly turned this down to the level of her umbilicus (navel), and then stepped back awaiting the student's examination.

Methodically the student began the examination of this attractive woman, now undressed from the crown of her head to her mid-abdomen. First came the visual examination. He observed for any unusual heaves (rhythmic lift of the chest wall with the heartbeat) or abnormal contour in her rib cage, which might signal prolonged enlargement of her heart. In appropriate sequence, he placed the open palm of his hand over her left mid-rib cage just beneath her left breast. He gently pushed her breast upward as he attempted to identify any abnormal thrust or "thrill" (please excuse this embarrassing but correct nomenclature denoting a palpable vibration) conducted from the heart through the chest wall.

Having completed this part of the examination, he reached down for the bell of his stethoscope which hung professionally from his neck. He first methodically placed the bell of the stethoscope over the mitral valve area at the apex (tip) of the heart, about five centimeters from the left border of the sternum (breast bone) in the fifth intercostal space (ICS = space between the ribs).

After pausing here for some time, he moved the stethoscope along the ICS space to the left border of the sternum and then slowly upward along the left sternal margin until he arrived at the pulmonic valve area in the second left intercostal space. He then moved along laterally to the second intercostal space on the right to listen for any associated abnormalities in the aortic valve.

It was after this rather extended period of seeming auscultation (listening) that the young woman reached up to the student physician's neck, grasped the ear pieces of his stethoscope still clinging around his neck, and placed them in his ears. His color most assuredly resembled my classmate's at that point.

The Plumbing Department

The Urology Department at the University of Iowa was another area where rather timid young medical students were "toughened up." We commonly referred to it as the "plumbing department." Because of the "gross" nature of the anatomic parts dealt with in this subspecialty, the language used to convey information similarly tended to be a bit gross.

Dr. Culp, the assistant department head, instructed us to deal with the delicateness of the subject matter in a manner appropriate to the patient with whom we were dealing. He said, "Don't ask an aging Iowa farmer, 'Do you have difficulty voiding?' Ask him if he 'can piss over a three-rail fence' or if he 'dribbles on his shoes.' " I might add that I was pleased to find that I felt equally comfortable with those who pissed, passed water, urinated or voided.

Unpleasantries Necessary

The late Rubin Flocks, who was the head of the same urology department, stressed to us in the classroom that something as simple, and yet unpleasant for the patient and the doctor, as a rectal examination could yield an early and perhaps life-saving diagnosis. This could be either a prostatic cancer or a malignancy of the rectum. I can still hear him screaming to the class, "There are only two contraindications to a rectal exam: One, no finger! Two, no rectum!"

Becoming "at ease" in one's personal clinical arena seems to me to entail a combination of firsthand experiences, listening to clinical anecdotes and at times trial and error until the "pathway of least resistance" becomes clear.

▪ CHAPTER 16 ▪

The Art of Grasping the Fat Lady

As I LAUNCH out on the task of summarizing my course in life from birth through my career preparation, I am reminded of several educational as well as challenging experiences. This particular episode occurred when I was a Medical Nurse Assistant (MNA) the summer after my second year of medical school at the University of Iowa.

An MNA at the University of Iowa in the 1960s was a person who had completed two years of medical school. Such a person was eligible to work at the University hospitals as a "glorified orderly." In today's market, it would be similar to the responsibilities of a licensed practical nurse. Given a special orientation, and considering our basic sciences and pharmacy education, we could pass "meds."

While trying to earn some money between my sophomore and junior year of medical school, I worked as a MNA on one of the female medical wards. This particular day, I was busy working at the end of the ward nearest the nurses' station. A patient in the middle of the room pulled the curtain around her bed to do something private (the curtains around the bed was the only privacy a patient had on a ward in those days). It later became clear that she had put her bed pan on the edge of the bed to void. At the completion of her task, she tried to get off the bed, and in doing so she knocked the stainless steel bed pan off the edge of her bed onto the floor with a loud metallic bang and an audible splash.

She next tried to retrieve the spilled pan. She slid off the bed, down onto the now very wet floor, which was marble and very slick, and fate unfolded. Needless to say, splash/bang was followed by an inevitable wet thud.

I hurried with the remainder of the nursing staff to the point of the incident. Pulling back the curtain, we found a very short, obese and naked lady, probably four foot eleven inches tall and weighing 250 pounds, sitting helplessly on the floor in a pool of urine with the metal bed pan nearby. Beyond her pride, she denied being hurt.

Initially, there were several failed attempts by the nurses to have her take hold of their arms so they could pull her up. These efforts only led to her feet sliding out again and repeatedly flopping back on the hard, wet marble floor.

As the only man in the group gathered around her bed to assist, I was faced with the age-old question, "Where does one take a hold of a fat lady when you want to lift her, in this case, from a pool of urine?" The problem was magnified by the fact that she was wet from ear to toe and as slick as a greased pig.

After surveying the situation for a time, I elected to squat down beside this seriously obese woman, allow her to lock her arms around my neck and then stand straight up with this naked glob of wet humanity draping against me while her bare feet slipped and slid on the hard wet floor beneath us. By keeping my feet squarely beneath me and going from a squatting to a standing position, I was able to bring her to a vertical (standing) position.

Once she was delivered safely back to her bed, I hurried off to exchange my urine-soaked white uniform for a clean, dry scrub suit.

Perhaps the "Art" was in NOT "grasping" the Fat Lady!

CHAPTER 17

The Art of Being Physician and Friend

WHILE SERVING MY junior medical student rotation on the female medicine ward, I first experienced caring for someone I knew very well. S.W. and I rode the same school bus all through our high school years. I saw her daily in the hallways, participated with her in school events, and knew her family.

After high school, I left home to attend college, married my last year in college, weathered three years in the military service, had two daughters while in the service and finally achieved my goal of becoming a medical student. My high school friend married directly after high school, lived on a farm, and had daughters about the same age as my two girls.

After a period of nearly 10 years, I was struck by the coincidence of S.W. being admitted to the same female ward to which I was assigned. Second, I was further surprised to find that out of five ward clerks (third-year medical students), she happened to fall to my care on natural rotation. Third, I was jolted by her state of health. She had lost a considerable amount of weight, was spiking temperatures to 105 degrees, and was exceedingly weak and lethargic.

On my tier one exam, I found Sharon had marked lymphadenopathy (enlarged lymph glands) in her neck. Several biopsies had been taken as an outpatient. Reed-Sternberg cells were finally found in her last lymph node biopsy. This established the definitive diagnosis of Hodgkin's Disease (a specific type of lymphoma).

Now realizing that I was initiating the first step of her six-tier work-up, I felt apologetic for the contribution she was required to make to my medical education. Besides feeling emotionally connected to her as a friend and schoolmate, she represented my first experience caring for a patient with Hodgkin's Disease. I felt a sense of guilt as I initiated what I knew would be a series of uncomfortable examinations in the face of her grave illness and our pre-existing friendship.

Sharon accepted the system graciously. It was only after she weathered the multiple-tiered examinations, received treatments of nitrogen mustard, prednisone, irradiation and experienced the resolution of her fever and dissolution of the enlarged lymph nodes that I began to feel that maybe the system was okay.

At this juncture, I realized that I could be a physician *and* a friend. I could serve to inform and console the family and bring a bit of cheer to a condition for which there would be little lasting cheer. At the time there was not the hope of a long-term cure for Hodgkin's Disease, as there is today.

Her disease was in a guarded "remission." Sharon was dismissed from the acute care ward, to be followed as an outpatient in the hematology clinic. Periodically I received lay progress reports through my mother, who shopped at the hometown grocery store where S.W.'s mother worked.

Another Encounter

Coincidence seemed to prevail. During my senior medical clerkship Sharon was again admitted to the female medical floor where I was assigned. Again, my friend became my patient and under my clinical care. Her disease had progressed. She now had other groups of involved lymph nodes in her groin and axillae. Again, Sharon patiently submitted to the multi-tiered work-up. The prednisone and mustard therapy was repeated and irradiation treatments were directed to the larger matted groups of lymph nodes. The therapy again led to a period of remission and again she returned home to her family.

Broadened Horizons

As my senior year came to an end, I traveled to Kansas City General Hospital where I hoped to, and did, find the weekly meetings of the "Knife and Gun Club" and the associated hands-on responsibility of an acute trauma center. Here, I also found the more liberal assignment of responsibility typical of a metropolitan institution with lesser funds and greater acute needs.

Having completed my rotating internship, I returned to my native Midwestern University of Iowa for what turned out to be a single year of internal medicine. During my internship year, I became interested in ENT, put in a single application to Mayo Clinic and was accepted. Thus, one year into my internal medicine residency, I switched to an otolaryngology (ENT) residency at what we referred to in Iowa as the "little clinic to the north."

Another Coincidence

My residency year in internal medicine saw no relaxation of the series of coincidences revolving around S.W.'s care. However, at this juncture I was somewhat less surprised when one day early in my female medicine rotation I again found S.W. on her way to what was now "my" female ward. This time I was not required to print the lengthy H&P. I didn't have to ask all the time-consuming questions that were inappropriate to her case. With a more experienced eye, I did see a young woman who no longer could be afforded the expectation of a short period of treatment and a long period of remission.

S.W. was ravaged by the repeated insults to her immune system administered with the hope of yet another remission from her devastating disease. Her face bore the typical "moon-faced" appearance that is a result of continued high doses of steroids (prednisone). Her body hair had fallen out because of numerous treatments of nitrogen mustard, and she wore a wig to avoid the embarrassment of female baldness. Her tongue and lips were cracked, sore and bleeding. She was barely more than skin and bones and had no appetite.

This time her grave illness only progressed rather than improving following her admission to the ward. She soon demonstrated progressive central nervous system signs. A spinal tap was carried out. Microorganisms were found in the spinal fluid documenting fungal meningitis, a common opportunistic infection resulting from prolonged immunosuppression. In this critical state, we moved her to a private room on the ward reserved for critically and terminally ill patients. Her course continued on a downward spiral, and she soon lapsed into a coma. The gravity of her condition worsened hourly.

Despite appropriate treatment for the infection, several afternoons later it became clear to those of us on the ward and those who consulted from the hematology and infectious disease services that S.W. could not last much longer.

By now, my relationship with her parents and her husband was much closer than with a typical brief treatment and short-stay type of patient. It was my responsibility to dispel the ever-present optimism of the dying patient's family and point out realistically that the time of her death was near at hand.

S.W.'s husband discussed the situation with her mother and me. He felt, and we agreed, that he should drive home that evening with the express purpose of telling their daughters, "Mother will not return home this time." S.W. had tried to prepare them for this moment, but was unable to explain that the time was very close. This became Dad's unhappy task.

Having two daughters of my own, I keenly grasped the magnitude of this young father's intended message to their children. I could not help but feel an outpouring of compassion. Believing and trusting in God, I felt compelled to pray. I asked that, in some way beyond my understanding, God would intervene in this most certain process of death. Yet, I acknowledged a will beyond mine which should be done.

The next morning S.W. awakened from her coma. She seemed as refreshed as one would from a restful sleep and was as lucid as I had seen her since the onset of her illness. She talked freely with her family and those of us who had cared for her that morning. That evening she lapsed back into an unconscious state and died.

If I had not surmised earlier, at that juncture I became acutely aware of a truism verbalized by Ambrose Pâre in the 16th century, "I treat, God heals." The art of medicine rests ultimately in the hands of the Supreme Being. My lot was to be a physician *and* a friend.

■ CHAPTER 18 ■

The Art of Glib Rounds

PRIOR TO THE government's interpretation of human rights requiring semiprivate rooms for Medicare patients, most indigent patients — those living below the poverty level — except for the very ill and those afflicted with a contagious illness, were placed in "open wards." This now outdated arrangement required less nursing personnel and certainly less physical nursing effort, while still keeping close watch on a large number of patients.

In an open ward, patients on either side of and directly across from gravely ill patients anxiously sounded the alarm whenever the acutely ill patient was in distress. However, because of this arrangement, with so many patients being located in close proximity, medical rounds became a bit of a game to see how well the staff could communicate in a language heard by all within earshot on the ward and yet understood only by those on the medical team.

In my personal experience, about one-third of the patients at any given time were being evaluated for symptoms likely related to serious disease entities, while the remainder had less acute illnesses often propagated by psychosocial problems. During this more liberal admission period in medical history, the work-up was designed to rule out (or in) significant medical ailments.

With tongue in cheek, I must admit that we occasionally stood at the bed of a flagrant violator of true medical illness and allowed our verbal imaginations to roam. For example, an intern or resident might turn to the group in a somber and yet casual way and report that a patient's serum porcelain level (not something tested for in the lab) was significantly elevated. Because this hypothetical level was included in a list of otherwise normal test results, nothing was suspected by those outside of the group at the foot of the bed. If the violator was even more flagrant, the resident might be heard to announce in a casual flowing manner that this particular "cycloceramic" (in both cases referring to a "crock") patient should soon be ready for dismissal.

A real grasp of the art was the ability to stand at the foot of the patient's bed and discuss the entire case without the patient understanding one bit of what was being said. I sometimes wonder if this bit of verbal gymnastics did not account for the origin of some of the awe in patient-physician relationships.

At the bedside, bits and pieces of the history would be repeated in a serious tone of voice. Totally inaccurate conclusions conjured up by the patient would be recounted as fact. Such statements as, "She has an essentially positive history and review of systems," would further support the case for no physical disease. Positive here carries the double meaning that the patient would grasp at every suggested symptom as indeed being a part of their personal medical symptomatology.

Not uncommonly, these patients were synthetic enough that they were already identified by their patient peers. As physicians, we noted what we felt were other tell-tale markers, such as the female patient with gold bedroom slippers under her bed. Gold or silver slippers under a female patient's bed seemed pathognomonic for that patient being neurotic.

Today third-party payers have demanded a dramatic reduction in the number of in-hospital evaluations of "cycloceramics." However, I suspect that even today students of medicine have the occasional need to be glib.

■ CHAPTER 19 ■

The Art of Caring for
Those Far from Home

GUSTA LOGES CAME to the University Hospital in the early 1960s with a number of health problems that needed attention. Foremost was regulating her adult onset but insulin-dependent diabetes which had gotten out of hand.

Gusta's problems were magnified by the fact that she had bilateral advanced cataracts that had rendered her legally blind the last 10 years. She was a spinster with no family and was able to live alone because she had lived in her tiny home so long she knew every inch of it by feel. She was a wonderful neighbor and friend to everyone in her neighborhood, when she was able. She invited children into her home for goodies, made hand-worked gifts for tokens of friendship and prepared special dishes for those who were ill. Now it was time for paybacks, and her neighbors were delighted to be of assistance.

The deterioration of her own health and the inability to care for herself was very depressing to Gusta. She expressed her desire to just allow nature to take its course. As her third-year medical student, I was pleased to contribute my part to Gusta's multi-tiered care. Her clinical assessment revealed that she was in better health than one would have initially surmised. Her diabetes did present a problem because her lack of vision required that the insulin be drawn up and prepared by someone else. She was sent for an ophthalmology consult, and it was felt that she merely had mature cataracts that could be cared for surgically.

Gusta had always been "healthy as a horse" and in her state of mind was not interested in any kind of surgery. I took it upon myself to become part of her support group while she was away from home. I spent a lot of extracurricular time visiting with her about her home, her friends and the future. While she was still negative about any kind of surgery, I began telling her that once she had her eye surgery, "The grass would never be greener nor the sky bluer."

We became good friends. After church one Sunday, I brought my wife and two daughters by the hospital to meet her and to assure her that wherever she went she did have friends. In those days, hospital stays were long enough one was able to become a trusted friend to some patients. In Iowa, patients would come from across the state via the university ambulance system and remained until their needs had been met. This was the case with Gusta. She finally agreed to schedule cataract surgery and to return to the University Hospitals via the well-known Iowa ambulance system.

I can still remember going to the ward Sunday after she had her first surgery. We were on the way home from church. I put Gusta in a wheelchair and took her to the hospital's central lobby to meet Marge and my daughters, who were too small to be allowed on the ward. She had a patch over her operated eye. The patch had been removed, the eye checked and the patch replaced the day before by her ophthalmologist. All was going well. Nothing would do but I help untape the eye patch so she could have her first glimpse of me and my family. She was overjoyed as she laughed and hugged each of us. Until that moment, we had only been voices in the dark.

She would require refraction for better vision since lens implants were not on the scene as yet, but what she could see of us must have been a wonderful improvement. She was not only elated, but momentarily ready to schedule a time to come back for surgery on her other eye. Over the remainder of my junior year and during my senior year, each time Gusta returned, we were her family. During her last visit that year, we were able to get a pass for her and take her to church, where I was campus pastor for the small congregation.

My continued training took us out of Iowa to first Missouri and then Minnesota. However, with her newfound vision, Gusta was able to write to us regularly for another decade. She sent our daughters items of handwork which she was able to resume making because of her improved vision.

She trusted me when I told her that the grass would never be greener and the sky never bluer than after she had her eye surgery. What I hadn't realized was that those colors deepened and became more vivid for my entire family as well, because we shared with Gusta.

▪ CHAPTER 20 ▪

The Art of Renewal

FOR THE FARMER who labors in the field, the laborer in industry, the mother in the home and the professional in his/her practice, renewal may simply mean a good night's rest. For the seasonal plants and trees, it may mean a time to gather nutrients, to flower, to form seeds, and then to lay dormant for a time before spring brings new buds, new leaves, new seeds and finally new seedlings. For the human animal species, renewal is caught up in all of the above. But it is also caught up in replenishing our own kind through the birthing process.

Forty years ago, when I launched off into the art of medicine, birthing, as today, was generally a joyful part of the art of medicine. Most babies were born healthy, most mothers did well and the legal community at that point was not practicing medicine. Some of my most memorable experiences in medical education came in the birthing arena where human renewal came in the form of a "brand spanking" new baby.

Getting Acquainted with Renewal

During our senior year as medical students, five of us rotated through obstetrics for two weeks at a time. We learned to examine the mother, stage the progress of delivery and monitor, although crudely, the progress of the baby. With appropriate supervision, I was allowed to deliver 12 babies of multiparous (two or more pregnancies) mothers and monitor the progress of many women who were having their first baby ("primips").

Although I was credited with the assist, I had little to do with the delivery of the first mother I followed. She was pregnant with her 17th child. Needless to say, she could teach me much more than I could help her. In fact, when she started having contractions with regularity, and her dilation was approaching six centimeters, the nurse and I started moving her bed toward the delivery room. As we were pushing the bed through the door, she simply gave a couple of small grunts, and there was a baby in the bed right in the doorway to the delivery room.

The process was not a new one for me. I sat many cold nights in the barn while sows farrowed and cows calved. I had no difficulty promptly clearing the baby from the membranes and fluid before moving the mother into the room to deliver the placenta.

At the other end of the spectrum, one of my more memorable experiences was sitting with a 19-year-old unmarried primiparous (first pregnancy) woman who was accompanied by her mother. She had been moved to the university from one of the indigent maternity clinics sponsored by the university in her hometown of Centerville. Several such facilities were located around the state.

I seemed to bond well with both her and her mother. This relationship may have been cultivated by the fact that she came from the same town where a number of my mother's family still resided. At this point, I was 30 years old, had been through two pregnancies with my wife and was open and understanding about the predicament in which this young woman found herself. I sensed the understandable anxiety of this mother-to-be. First, there was the fear of the birthing process. Second, she was embarrassed to lean on the support of her parents (mother in the final hours). Third, this was the first time she would be required to be primarily responsible for such a small child (who just happened not to have the name of its father).

My early relationship consisted of small talk and a bit of personal philosophy. However, each time I visited the labor room to check on her, I shared a joke. I love to tell jokes and have difficulty forgetting those I hear. In the early 1960s elephant jokes were in vogue. For example:

Question: "Why do elephants have flat feet?" Answer: "Your feet would be flat, too, if you were pregnant for two years."

This routine predictably went on for hours, as is the case in primips. There was more time to vent, to philosophize and to appreciate the miracle of birth. Labor progressed well; a healthy baby girl was the ensuing product. Baby, mom and grandmother all returned to southern Iowa in good health. Beyond remembering this friendly encounter, somewhere in my archives I have a letter from this teenager's mother giving me a progress report on the young mother and her child. Mother thanked me for helping turn a family crisis, and a personal one for her daughter, into a memorable, meaningful and joyful experience.

Renew in Volume

Sometimes renewal comes with little thought or preparation. Such was the case a year later during internship. My OB experience at General Hospital was approximately tenfold that of my medical school rotation, in number, and held a proportional allotment of memorable experiences.

In a city hospital many impending deliveries come through the emergency room door with no prenatal care. To top my senior medical student delivery experience in a doorway, I delivered a woman in an elevator at the Kansas City General Hospital. Pregnant women coming through the emergency room were checked for stage of labor. Those who were minimally dilated were asked to leave, walk around for a time, and come back later to be rechecked when the contractions were stronger and closer together.

One evening, as I was about to leave after my 6 a.m. to 6 p.m. shift in the emergency room, a woman came through the ambulance door in hard labor. We had two delivery packs of sterile instruments and stirrups for the ER tables ready to go if needed. Instead of using one of the packs and proceeding with a delivery in the ER, the second shift intern talked me into putting the woman on a gurney and rushing her around the halls of the u-shaped building to the end of the opposite wing where an elevator would take us down two floors to the labor and delivery suite. Supposedly, I could then go on home.

Needless to say, the woman began sustained pushing the moment the elevator doors closed. By the time the rather slow and antiquated elevator stopped and the doors opened, there were three of us in the elevator. The appropriate niceties were carried out on the spot, and the placenta was delivered a few minutes later in the delivery suite. Mother and baby were fine.

During OB rotation, we were on call and slept on the ward every other night and spent every day in the unit. When interns were not following the women in labor, we could read and study more about the "what ifs." One of the subjects that caused me some concern was a breach birth delivery. I took special note as to the hemline methodology of caring for such an event.

Upside Down Renewal

Again, we were practicing medicine in an era before lawyers and insurance companies also practiced, or second-guessed medical care and fear dictated routine C-sections for breach deliveries. I was acquainted with low forceps deliveries and quite well informed on the usual types of emergencies. The interns' quarters consisted of a locker and bunk bed right in the delivery suite. The resident on call slept in a special suite, or quarters, in one of the towers some distance and a number of minutes away. These semi-comfortable rooms were provided for house staff members in each of the many different specialties. A pool table, TV and snacks made these quarters more comfortable.

It was not uncommon to be summoned quickly to a delivery room without as much as the benefit of slipping into one's shoes. There were two particular times during my month-long stint when I was urgently summoned for the delivery of women in the final stages of labor without the benefit of a prenatal work-up or care. In each case, the woman was pregnant with twins.

The first baby was delivered uneventfully, but when the fundus of the uterus remained abnormally prominent, a quick exam revealed a foot at the cervical os. The textbooks at that time described this as a time for immediate action. The second foot was sought, identified and pulled down through the cervix (version) and a gentle tug was maintained with the next contraction (extraction). By rotating the baby's torso forward to flex the neck, the second child was delivered without incident. In both cases, my quick burst of adrenaline allowed me an appropriately hasty second delivery before the cervix contracted down. Thus, we had two gravida 2 para 1 situations with four healthy babies (four conceptions delivered through two cervixes dilated only once).

Needless to say, in each case I had an upset resident the following morning. Twins were known to be the resident's domain. They, however, had no reason for criticism or recourse. The time it would have taken for them to get up, get dressed and get to the delivery suite would have precluded the opportunity of a safe vaginal delivery. To date, I haven't met another ENT specialist who has delivered two sets of twins vaginally, particularly when one in each case is breach. In fact, few young obstetricians have done so in an environment where lawyers and C-sections are in vogue.

Renewal with Alternatives

As interns, we were expected to deliver uncomplicated primiparous women. One young woman who arrived on the labor ward was a 15-year-old African-American girl whose mother I had cared for in the medicine clinic. The mother, Mary, had severe rheumatic heart disease. With Mary's last pregnancy, she developed congestive heart failure, coded and miraculously was resuscitated. She and the baby both survived. She had been told that another pregnancy might be fatal. However, fertility and sensuality won out over fear and common sense. She, too, was being monitored closely through yet another pregnancy. We were frustrated by Mary, but we all loved and cared for her. Being both chronically ill and pregnant so often, she became "family" to both the medical and obstetrical staff.

As I introduced myself to Mary's daughter, I spoke to her about the fondness we all felt for her mother. I then talked a bit about her own pregnancy out of wedlock. Having a number of younger brothers and sisters, she wanted to keep her child rather than putting it up for adoption.

After checking her progress a few times, it became apparent that the labor was not going to progress rapidly. As I thought about her circumstance, I remembered my medical school rotation on psychiatry. We had learned a technique of suggestion (or hypnosis). This involved a step-wise combination of numbers and progressive images carried out sequentially until the patient was completely relaxed and open to suggestion. I decided to ask her permission to try this technique and she consented.

Once she was in a receptive mode, I suggested that she relax and sleep as her labor progressed. She was to feel pressure but no pain. I assured her that when delivery was imminent, we would put a small needle in her back with a numbing medicine. This "spinal" would allow delivery without pain.

The labor ward was set up with beds on both sides of the

aisle. The nurses went up and down the aisle every 15 minutes or so and lifted the sheets which were draped over strap metal tents. These arched over the expectant mother's pelvic area and facilitated checking each patient's progress. Mary's daughter slept for two to three hours without rousing. Then on one of the routine sequential checks, the nurse exclaimed with great surprise, "She's crowning!" (The cervix was near complete dilatation and the crown of the baby's head was well visualized.) Because I had promised the spinal, and I did not want to risk breaking the trust I had established with her, I quickly and uneventfully administered the spinal. She proceeded to deliver, never once complaining of pain. I was never quite sure of the formula for this experience, but it seemed to be based on a strong bond of trust and full acceptance of suggestion. I have always wondered what would have happened if I had carried the suggestion completely through delivery without the spinal.

Accumulated Renewal

The "war stories" from those learning situations are legion, but somehow each experience contributed to my ability to practice the art of medicine.

Other stories are also memorable because of their "gee whiz" value — such as the 13-year-old girl undergoing her second C-section for as many pregnancies, and the woman who arrived in the emergency room with a baby retrieved from the toilet stool. The latter thought she was having a bowel movement (unrecognized labor). The baby did acquire pneumonitis but survived.

To me, this period of medicine was a wonderful time. The rewards of appreciative patients were coupled with the joys of learning. The practice of medicine was exciting, exhilarating and fortunately *not* smothered by bureaucracy and impeded with the fear of lawsuits (a subject for a future book).

▪ CHAPTER 21 ▪

The Art of Appropriate Compassion

THE ETHICS AND morality of the medical profession is something which, in my mind, verges on being sacred. In days past, broken doctor-patient relationships could mean the loss of respect and socioeconomic clout. Today, such violations could cost the farm (or one's estate), as well as one's license to practice. I have always believed that safeguards toward this end begin with our attire and are reinforced by careful avoidance of inappropriate interpersonal risks.

A dress shirt, tie and white lab coat go a long way toward describing the appropriate emotional distance between a physician and the patient. Appropriate and acceptable conversation similarly commands a professional distance, particularly important during the physical examination. The continuous presence of staff members during an exam of the opposite gender has always been appropriate (in the current environment, an absolute essential). Today, this may be true for the same gender.

Despite a uniform effort to maintain professional distance, I had one experience during my rotating internship that involved a female patient who made repetitive and unsolicited efforts to become intimate.

To the best of my knowledge, I did nothing to instigate or encourage an unethical relationship. I merely proceeded with my customary effort to be kind, gentle and understanding. Immediately after her first inappropriate attention and effort to go beyond the usual doctor-patient relationship, I shared this problem with my wife. From this point on, I found it convenient to arrange every subsequent medical visit (real or feigned) to be carried out by one of my classmates (having first assessed them of the situation well in advance).

I had delivered this woman's second child, the product of a second failed marriage. After treating her with no more than the usual kindness, I first received a letter of appreciation for the good care I had provided during her hospital stay. This would have been both appropriate and adequate. However, she then began calling for additional postpartum appointments with rather "weak excuses," or at most, vague reasons.

After receiving a second letter now encouraging a romantic involvement, I promptly saw to it that I had no further contact with this woman. Despite my efforts to avoid her, she paged me numerous times at the hospital and continued with a series of letters, each more insistent on an illicit affair than the prior. One of the later correspondences delivered to the hospital mail room included a nude self-portrait (she was quite an accomplished artist) of her being cradled by a tiger. However, with what seemed to be appropriate and timely efforts to discourage her advances, she wrote one final desperate letter, and then apparently moved on to more fertile ground.

The woman was very attractive, artistic, obviously well educated, and at one time had money. Fortunately for me, I anticipated a "fatal attraction" personality and seemingly chose a workable solution to the problem. My wife and I both mused about how fortunate we were that no encouragement was offered. The many unanswered letters were accompanied by newspaper articles journaling her divorce, the family players on both sides, and the apparent "high society" from which she was expelled.

I placed the trappings of this epistle into a file, which I promised would one day be a chapter in my book. It remains in my drawer as evidence of one more lesson in the art of medicine.

As I now go back and revisit the memories of her rather torrid pursuit, my eye catches a self-diagnosis of this woman's personality, where she apologized for being a "schizo-manic-depressive." Fatal attractions, unfortunately, may be brewing totally unbeknownst to a physician. Thus, while continuing to be compassionate toward patients, medical professionals must be perpetually careful that compassion is not misinterpreted by a psychologically unstable patient as an inappropriate act of passion. When this does occur, prompt and effective distance must be established between the physician and the troubled patient.

At the time, the problem seemed to be only a significant nuisance. After movies such as *Fatal Attraction,* and hearing about similar instances of both bizarre and threatening circumstances, we should perhaps have been more fearful then, and more thankful now.

CHAPTER 22

The Art of Fair Play (and Abusing Same)

SERVICES AT THE old Kansas City General Hospital in the 1960s were made possible by the large staff of interns, a relatively smaller cadre of residents in the specialties and a generous teaching staff of dedicated community physicians.

The emergency room, the first "line of defense" in the medical and surgical care arena, was manned by a full complement of interns (29 in my internship year). Each year this extremely important "professional" commodity had to be replenished.

One recruiting technique was the telling of "war stories," with great relish. As we concluded our year as interns and prepared to go into practice (as general practitioners did after internship in those days), or return to the "Ivory Tower" (university settings) for further training, promotional talks were arranged to undergraduate classes at our alma maters. Our intent was to encourage those who were exploring internship possibilities to come to Kansas City General Hospital.

As a junior and senior medical student, I heard many "war stories" about the number of deliveries an intern could expect, the direct responsibility handed over to interns and the amount of trauma care assigned to interns. These were the fruits — the challenges — we had longed for during years of close medical supervision. These "war stories" were enough to whet the appetite of students sheltered by the orderly and very supervised learning process available to medical students in Midwestern universities.

Other than farm accidents, I had experienced very little trauma, and even less violent trauma in medical school. I also experienced a much lower incidence of indigent pregnancies and much closer supervision than in an inner-city general hospital. Besides those from the University of Iowa, our internship class was filled with graduating medical students from the University of Missouri at Columbia, University of Nebraska and Kansas University in Kansas City, Kansas.

Despite these "built-in attractions," recruiting was still required to fill such large internship classes. Therefore, we interns were encouraged to visit our alma maters at appointed times and to meet with the graduating class.

A relatively small sum of money was set aside by General Hospital to be utilized for this purpose. It was available on a first-come, first-serve basis until the fund was depleted. Interns who had cause to "go home" did so gladly for no more than the chance to get away from the grueling schedule.

Needless to say, a couple of the "guys" (no women in our internship class) were streetwise beyond their years — and devoid of the farm boy ethics of us rural students. They were the first to come forward with a plan for a formal recruiting trip to a more distant medical school — Denver, Colorado.

They received a naively open IOU from the Internship Recruiting Fund accountant and planned an extensive trip early in the school year. Before the rest of us knew what was happening, this dynamic duo submitted receipts that gobbled up the entire fund. Their unwise, undisciplined "recruiting" with wine, women and song netted no new interns for the next class, but produced great tales of their escapades, avoidance of a week's work, and an unfairly depleted recruitment fund.

The remainder of my class had to dip into their own pockets to recruit. In most cases, all we could afford was to meet briefly with the medical school classes when we happened to return home. There was no wine, women and song — or even dinner and lodging.

The leader of this pair (we'll call him Jim) was married, fashioned himself a playboy and would delight in saying, "I want to do what's right — for me!" This "one in every class" intern had family responsibilities; however, he was the only class member I recall who openly and chronically "chased skirts" (usually the naïve nursing students who were near at hand and driven by an abundance of hormones).

Jim not uncommonly asked classmates to cover for him while he "played." He would instruct his peers, "If my wife calls, tell her I'm out on the ward doing a procedure on a patient." Instead, he would be having a short fling with a willing "cutie" away from the hospital.

Although one would hope that somewhere along in his training he would learn the significance of his professional oath, I am afraid this is most likely optimistic and he would more likely meet with his wife's lawyer and the Board of Healing Arts.

This experience was a negative lesson in ethics, interpersonal relations and maturing in medicine; however, it did prepare me for service work on hospital bylaws, ethics and executive committees.

■ CHAPTER 23 ■

The Art of Rationing

IN THE EARLY 1960s, the University of Iowa Hospitals' first hemodialysis unit demanded and claimed its rightful position in the center of a top-floor suite in the main University Hospital building. A peculiar mystique hovered over our compact group of five students, the resident, and our staff physician as we completed rounds and anxiously sought our first glimpse of the machinery that had the potential to prolong and possibly save the lives of patients with renal (kidney) failure.

My first glimpse of the unit immediately reminded me of a stainless steel replica of my mother's Speed Queen agitator washing machine. The uniqueness of the unit, coupled with the feeling of awe as we contemplated its potential feats, caused us all to cautiously, if not fearfully, examine the vat and its content.

The professor exuded complete knowledge and command of the instrument as he removed the hinged lid that covered the vat. He explained the principle involved in the movement of crystalloids through a filtering membrane impermeable to colloids. At this juncture in time, with this unit, only one or two patients could be dialyzed per day. The rumored figure of $1,300 (a large sum of money in 1963) for each cleansing of a patient's blood registered as a shocking amount of money to this country boy reared well beneath the poverty level.

Who would reap the benefit of this startling new technology?

Sarah

Back on the women's ward, occupying the first bed on the left, was a young woman I'll call "Sarah." Sarah was 17 years old with diagnosed end-stage renal disease. Sarah had suffered with chronic nephritis since she was a little girl. Her kidneys were now barely functioning. Despite the fact that she was extremely careful about what she ate, drank and took in the way of medication, her kidneys could no longer filter her metabolic waste products.

Sarah retained fluids, and her blood pressure soared despite anti-hypertensives. Thick glasses functioned poorly reflecting her retinal devastation, only one of the many sequela of her ongoing hypertension.

As a student, I internalized an urgency to do something definitive for this pleasant young woman. She, however, appeared collected and resigned to her destiny — as did our more mature staff. When we asked, "Can Sarah somehow be dramatically saved by the wonderful new machine upstairs?" "No," we were told. "Sarah's disease is end-stage. Her kidneys will not get better, and it would be far too expensive to maintain her on hemodialysis."

For Sarah, the only choice was to let her go, or start her on peritoneal dialysis. Being young, personable and a real little scrapper, Sarah was afforded chronic peritoneal dialysis. Under local anesthesia, a one-centimeter scalpel incision was made through her skin into the sparse subcutaneous fatty tissue on Sarah's abdomen. Through this incision a brutal-appearing trocar was forced into her abdominal cavity. Two liters of dialysate gurgled via gravity flow through a tube five times the size of an intravenous tube into Sarah's abdominal cavity. Every eight hours her tense tummy was decompressed through the siphon formed by lowering the bottle below her body. Promptly, her abdomen was again refilled to a pregnant-appearing state with fresh dialysate.

Despite this labor-intensive, and very restrictive existence, Sarah daily slipped closer to her ultimate demise.

Debbie

During this same time frame, six beds down the ward, lay another young woman we will call "Debbie." Debbie was 19 years old. This beautiful auburn-haired lass, in contrast to Sarah, was acutely ill.

Sensing more parental restrictions than she felt a young woman should experience, she and her boyfriend "ran away" to California. Long on romance and short on funds, Debbie did not have enough money to see a physician and buy penicillin, the appropriate medicine for the Strep sore throat she acquired shortly after arriving in California. The following week, she developed systemic symptoms with fever and chills, malaise, mylagia and then bloody urine with pain on voiding.

Literally and figuratively "sick," Debbie called home for help. Her family promptly arranged for her to return directly to the university hospital. I will never forget witnessing the now haunting and tearful reunion which took place as this bed-ridden and seriously ill young woman and her mother embraced for the first time following her return.

Again, we somewhat persistent, naive students forced the question, "Debbie must surely be a candidate for the dialysis machine?"

This time we were informed that when treated medically, about 80 percent of the patients with acute glomerulonephritis recover. Denying Debbie dialysis meant freeing up direly needed time on the dialysis machine for other patients perhaps more needy and appropriate.

However, in Debbie's case, the statistics did not work out. Debbie became progressively more ill. The waste products built up rapidly in her body and she became obtunded. A bleeding diaphysis occurred. Bruises appeared everywhere, probably including her brain. In a matter of days, she deteriorated abruptly and literally died in her mother's arms.

VA Selection

Three years later, I returned to the University of Iowa for my first year in the internal medicine residency program. One rotation assigned me to a male medical ward at the affiliated VA Hospital in Iowa City. In those few years after medical school, hemodialysis had expanded explosively. Federal funding afforded the VA Hospital an edge with more dialysis units than the state institution could afford. My assigned ward had the awesome responsibility of evaluating veterans with renal disease and selecting those to be offered regular hemodialysis.

I vividly recall the first candidate who came to my ward. This veteran, we'll call "Joe," was a young married schoolteacher with a young family. He was totally unaware of having renal disease until he experienced progressive fatigue, fluid retention and diminished urinary output. He made an appointment with his doctor. When evaluated by his primary care physician, it became apparent that he was in renal failure, and he was referred to the VA Hospital.

After appropriate lab work, including renal function studies, Joe went before the Chronic Dialysis Selection Committee. Joe was fortunate; he succeeded in being placed on the list for chronic dialysis.

Why Joe?

First, he had few of the complications of long-term renal disease. Second, he had an education that allowed him to be productive and provide for his family as a teacher at a relatively low-energy level. Third, he lived close enough that he could drive to the VA Hospital three nights a week and actually sleep while being dialyzed. After each dialysis, he would still be able to drive home before school resumed that day.

Other veterans were older. Some could only do very physically demanding work. They could not get to the dialysis unit while maintaining their current jobs. At a time when the slots available for dialysis were at such a premium, they could not be accepted into the program. Their destiny was sealed.

Ration?

To look back on these lives would cause one to characterize "rationing" as a consideration of cost, chance and circumstance. Without the item of cost and availability, Sarah's plight may have been modified at a time when she and her family could have looked beyond the painful 17th year when Sarah's struggles were finally ended and her family sensed deeply the emptiness surrounding her loss.

Debbie's plight revolved around one risk after another. With each spin of the wheel, each toss of the die, each dealing of the cards, she lost. First her family, then her health, and finally her life came into play. Her family returned to her life without hesitation. However, both the lover for whom Debbie risked it all and the deep love of her devoted family were snatched from her by that final decision to chance a spontaneous recovery.

The circumstances surrounding Joe's existence gave him a new lease on life. In contrast, the circumstances relative to the lives of many of the others competing for the same dialysis slots negated all hope for their treatment at that institution and at that time.

I dare say that as is the case in art forms, rationing is not an exact science, and it will continue to elude the desire for perfection. To some there will be joy; to others there will be haunting memories of what might have been if they could have been maintained until they recovered, or new technology gave renewed hope.

CHAPTER 24

The Art of "One-Upmanship"

"ONE-UPMANSHIP" IS a game common played in medical educational circles. Before our government legislated the big shift from wards to private and semiprivate rooms, indigent patients (who paid no hospitalization costs) and clinical pay patients (who paid for their room and medicines but *not* for physician care) were placed on wards. Again, the only exceptions to this rule were patients with contagious diseases, those with a need for intensive care and those so seriously ill that more private quarters were required to maintain dignity. It was on the wards that verbal heroics were commonplace, a stage for the drama to be played out.

Verbal Heroics

Emanating from the group of students and doctors who gathered three times a week to round with the attending staff doctor, there was always one or two of the group who would go to any extreme to impress the staff physician. Sometimes this would be one of the interns bucking for a fellowship. Other times it would be the resident who had particular interests in the subspecialty of the staff physician. Occasionally, it was just a hot-shot medical student who wished to stand out. Almost without fail, there would be at least one medical student who felt compelled to speak from a wealth of "inexperience."

Usually a brief overview of the major problems on the ward would be covered in the chart room, where every ward patient's record was stored in the chart rack. Here any decision that needed urgent early morning answers would be settled. Once this was done, the chart rack would be rolled out onto the ward. Rounds often started around 9 a.m. and the process would grind on tediously until close to noon. The resident-in-charge would often have a patient or two whom he was not ready to have the staff physician mull over extensively. Consequently, he would start the rounding process on the opposite side of the ward from the patients he wished to avoid.

Ulterior Motives

Some residents were quite skilled in bringing those patients up for discussion whose disease entities were close to the heart of the staff physician. In this way, the resident could stall the rounds early on so that the last part of the ward would be covered rather cursorily and his problem work-ups skipped over lightly, or not at all.

Various ulterior motives would prompt this type of "wardmanship." A prominent one was a delay in making an appropriate diagnosis. Another was avoiding a patient whom the resident physician just hadn't had enough time to study, research the literature and work up appropriately. It seemed to me that until a student reached his or her residency, this bit of inside understanding was not common knowledge. The staff physician should have been well aware of this little end play, but he was usually willing to trade off this bit of gamesmanship in order to be guided to the patients who provided him the best opportunity to expound on the subjects he knew and loved best.

The ward play was face-saving for the resident, impressive for the interns, and had a "gee whiz" factor for the students, who suspected the staff physician could expound equally well on all subjects.

When the resident knew that the staff physician had both strong and weak points, he knowingly tried to guide the rounding toward that staff person's personal expertise. At a later time, the resident could lean on fellow residents and staff in the subspecialties who could lend support that did not fall within the ward staff physician's forte. The rounds were also an opportunity for a good resident to give credit to either an outstanding intern or student workup.

Musing Over Patients

During my first-year residency in internal medicine, I often mused as I reviewed the patients on the ward and identified those whom I felt were truly in need of hospitalization versus those who were just there because of "their nerves."

Rounds began one morning in just such a setting with me being the resident-in-charge of the ward. I pushed the chart rack out from the nursing station and down in front of the first bed along the left side of the room. The majority of patients had by this time been through three tiers of their extensive medical evaluation: the extensive medical student work-up; the more selective intern evaluation; and the resident-level evaluation which I had performed.

The two interns, each responsible for half of the patients, were aboard and responsible for regurgitating a brief and concise version of the history provided by the patient. After that, they were prepared to summarize the pertinent physical findings, laboratory tests and the working diagnosis. Key conclusions and plans for further testing or treatment were outlined. We then discussed the stage of management at which we had arrived, in terms of both medical and physical treatment for that particular patient.

The Gunner

The intern's report was punctuated periodically by questions from the staff physician. Some questions were directed to the students and others to the intern. Generally, the resident-in-charge was politely assumed to know the matters being discussed. This was the juncture where the gunning medical student would have the opportunity to demonstrate how much midnight oil he had burned in order to answer the questions on which even the intern may stumble.

Not uncommonly, the same gunner would exhibit a verbal diarrhea pointed toward what he already knew was pertinent information (intelligent questions). Despite the staff physician's resistance, many "brownie points" could be gained by simply reading the staff physician's contributions to the medical literature (papers and editorial contributions) and regurgitating the points contained in these publications at the appropriate time. This bit of "one-upmanship" was always fodder for the rounding party's "gee whiz" guns.

On this particular day we had progressed about two-thirds of the way down the left row of beds. A large black woman, about 40 years of age, occupied the bed where the chart rack and accompanying entourage stopped. She was hospitalized because of essential hypertension which was out of control. This was a subject known to be dear to the attending physician's heart since much of his research work was in this area.

As we gathered at the foot of this woman's bed, the various causes of hypertension were discussed. Every consideration, from athrosclerosis and renal vascular abnormalities to inappropriate secretion of renin, was considered in detail. The "student gunner" dwelt for an eternity on the subject and poured out his guts on the relationship of renin (a substance produced by the kidney) to hypertension. Finally, as we concluded the subject of essential hypertension, particularly as it related to African-Americans, a short lull allowed the patient to wax philosophical. I might add as a footnote that throughout this entire conversation I was the only person who had not said a single word.

Looking directly at me and speaking in verbiage which

reflected her limited but insightful education, she said, "He knows sumpin' that the rest of ya don't know ... [long pause for emphasis] 'cause he ain't said nothin'."

Needless to say, the lesson I took away that morning did not come from the professor or any of his learned following regarding the subject of hypertension. In fact, the only patient I remember from rounds that day is the hypertensive black female patient. That morning she taught me that "one-upmanship" may at times be simply knowing when to keep one's mouth shut!

■ CHAPTER 25 ■

The Art of Cooking in Oil

WHILE PREVIOUSLY MENTIONING the university health care system in the 1960s, I indicated that a discussion of the clinical staff warranted a chapter(s) to itself. After reflecting for a while on some of those personalities, I'm afraid I need to sharpen that comment. Some individual staff members warrant a chapter unto themselves; others only need a paragraph or two in the sun. I particularly wish to address one person who we will refer to as Research Oriented (RO).

RO was recognized as an excellent researcher who was capable of acquiring voluminous quantities of research grant money in his sub-specialty area. I'm perhaps only slightly facetious when I say that I have always suspected that such distinguished recognition is largely based on one's ability to obtain grant money and having the tenacity to publish rather than to perish. As an aside, the reputation should rightfully be shared with the research assistants whose devotion and diligence allowed the work and grants to continue.

I need to point out once more that I am speaking of a "general" medicine ward. This means that the patients assigned to this ward could have any number of a myriad of internal medicine ailments. The ideal staff clinician and mentor, while possibly being most interested in one sub-specialty phase of internal medicine, would normally forego that personal bent and attempt to afford a well-rounded display of medical knowledge and teaching. RO, in my mind, was not this ideal clinician.

Once this somewhat militant being entered the ward from

the main corridor, the chart rack was pushed to the end of the ward and all hands were assembled in a "snap-to" fashion. Some staff clinicians would be patient enough to allow the medical students to present their individual cases as the group moved from bed to bed. Each case had the possibility of becoming a teaching experience for every person assigned to the ward.

This, however, was not RO's style. He merely wanted an extremely brief statement regarding the nature of the patient's problem, where we were in the workup and care program, and then it was off to the next bed. Occasionally, he would make an abrupt observation and, at times, a seemingly disjointed recommendation. This was the modus operandi until we happened to come to a patient with a problem in his specialty area. At that point, the chart rack came to a screeching halt, and there the process bogged down. Not uncommonly, the remainder of the allotted time would be spent discussing research models and seemingly esoteric minutiae.

Accepted SOP

The case of Hattie Smothers (fictitious name) best described the nature of this honestly rare obstacle in the normally excellent fifth tier of both medical education and patient care.

Hattie came to the ward with the progressive history of weakness and near-syncopal spells. At 70-plus years of age, it was suspected that she had significant atherosclerotic cerebrovascular disease. The changes in one's blood vessels at this age often do not allow for the person to go quickly from a lying or sitting position to an upright position without becoming light-headed. However, the severity of Hattie's symptoms and the progression of her fragile state caused the staff in the outpatient clinic to feel she deserved to be admitted for evaluation.

We had just received her initial admitting battery of tests when RO came to round with us on Monday morning. We breezed by the first five or six patients and came to Hattie. I, as the medical resident on the ward, briefly described Hattie's admission complaints. I then reported the only positive laboratory finding at the time was a depressed thyroid hormone level. I explained that, in accordance with the standard operating procedure (SOP) for a medical service, we planned a workup for panhypopituitarism.

To understand our plan, one must know that the pituitary gland, known commonly as the "master gland," is responsible for secreting hormones that regulate many target glands, including growth hormones, lactation, female reproductive organs, adrenal function, and the thyroid function. Depending on which portion of the pituitary gland is hypoactive, any target gland may fail to be stimulated by the master gland and necessarily become hypoactive as well.

When the adrenal gland is functioning normally, it responds to promptings from the pituitary gland. This is particularly true in stressful situations such as trauma, inflammatory illness and strenuous physical activity. At these times, cortisone-like products called corticosteroids are produced by the adrenal gland. When the pituitary gland fails to function, the adrenal glands also assume a sleeping state and are unable to respond acutely to stress. In this state, severe stress or injuries can lead to shock and possibly death.

It is common knowledge that thyroid hormone stimulates metabolism (the ill-advised reason many people have taken thyroid hormone to lose weight). When the hormone is administered inappropriately, it can be very stressful to the system. In an elderly patient, who may have a poorly or nonfunctioning pituitary gland, the stress of replacing the thyroid hormone without simultaneously administering replacement corticosteroids may throw the patient into acute cardiovascular collapse. My medical education at this point led me to heed the warning that the pituitary function should routinely be evaluated before treating one for severe hypothyroidism.

To accomplish this evaluation in the 1960s, one had to order an assay from a 24-hour urine collection. The intent of the assay was to determine the 24-hour corticosteroid levels and in this way the adrenal gland function in Hattie.

On this one particular morning rounds, RO rather flippantly suggested that I simply start Hattie on replacement thyroid hormone. I quietly resisted by pointing out that the 24-hour urines were being collected and that we hoped to do that soon.

When RO returned to round on Wednesday, Hattie was having more brief syncopal-like episodes and was seemingly a bit more confused as well. My gut feeling, plus my German stubbornness, caused me to choose insubordination a second time when a rather irate RO again directed me to "start her on thyroid!"

I again rather softly pointed out that we had some difficulty in the urine collection, but were still working on collecting the 24-hour urines. Only those of us who practiced medicine before the availability of the simple serum assays (blood studies) for corticosteroids will ever know the difficulty of collecting 24-hour urines. The collection fiasco was magnified many fold in patients who were disoriented and uncooperative. For those who have never attempted to collect 24-hour urine in a university hospital, that person would not understand the term "herding cats." With three shifts of personnel including nurses, aides, and orderlies, there was always at least one person who would forget to save the urine.

I further challenge anyone to explain to a confused female patient how she can go number two in the bedpan without going number one and messing up the whole sample. Nonetheless, as Thursday rolled around, we finally had accomplished the insurmountable task by placing signs on everything from the bed to the bedpan hopper (where stainless steel bedpans were emptied and steam cleaned). The specimen was forwarded to the lab, and we were awaiting the test results on Friday when RO returned to the floor.

On this day RO headed directly for Hattie's bed. Hattie was being almost as difficult as RO. She was even more confused and was generally weaker and, as is often stated, looked like "death warmed over."

When we arrived at her bed, RO abruptly asked if I had started her on thyroid. Rather than answering no, I apologetically stated that we had finally succeeded in collecting the 24-hour urine and that we expected the test results back that afternoon. In a blustery irate outburst in front of the interns, medical students and nurses, he shouted, "Hahn, if she dies, I'll personally boil your hide in oil!" With that, he stormed out of the ward without rounding further.

Hattie's tests did come back that afternoon. She did have panhypopituitarism. She was promptly but cautiously placed on an appropriate medical regimen including steroids and very low-dose, but progressively increasing level of thyroid hormone replacement. She soon perked up and was able to return home in a state fitting for her age.

During subsequent rounds, RO never acknowledged my clinical vindication, nor did he apologize for directing me to inappropriately treat and possibly cause Hattie's premature demise — or at least a "medical misadventure."

Someday I hope to visit RO in his lofty administrative office and ask if he still boils people in oil, or if he too has matured in medicine, along with the rest of us who rounded that day.

■ CHAPTER 26 ■

The Art of Altering a Training Program

I BOUNDED BRISKLY through the door, exiting stage left from the third floor University of Iowa Cardiovascular Conference Room and into the adjacent hallway. My exit was punctuated by the door banging closed behind me with a sound 25 dB (one normal hearing level) louder than necessary.

This conference room had ascending rows of seats equipped with headsets and phone jacks for listening to human heart sounds. Sometimes the sounds were taped; other times the amplified sounds were from a special stethoscope placed on a patient who had been wheeled to the front of the room on a gurney, or in a wheelchair. This room was also used as a general purpose conference room, including the general internal medicine conference which had just concluded as I so abruptly departed.

Each Friday afternoon at 4 p.m. two residents, pre-selected from the 15 or 20 residents in the entire program, were designated to present a half-hour discussion on an appropriate and timely subject. These subjects were usually suggested by the chief resident or one of the staff physicians.

Today was my day in the tank. I had just finished occupying the last half hour of this week's conference. I departed dramatically from the assigned topic and spoke instead to what I felt were glaring problems existing in the first-year medicine program. Most of these problems resulted from a beginning-of-the-year effort to revamp the program. The changes, designed to make the residency more appealing to the second and third year residents, were now being tested for the first time.

I paused for a moment in the south end of the third floor east wing hallway, a hallway that just now seemed at least a mile long. Behind me, the junction with the main axis, east-west corridor, formed at a right angle. The three medicine wards projected further to the south from the main hallway. Ahead of me was the long empty hallway leading to the north stairwell.

At this moment, I watched for the door I had allowed to slam shut to now burst open simultaneously with a second door at the left rear of the room. On a routine Friday afternoon, everyone in the packed room would pour into the hallway before the last word from the mouth of the second resident had faded. Today this did not occur.

After this extended pause, I began to walk slowly toward the far end of the lengthy hall. I passed the private offices and the neighboring laboratories. The hall seemed frighteningly empty. Not one soul ventured into the corridor as I walked along. Even the lab personnel and office staff were hauntingly inconspicuous.

With each measured step, I expected to hear the familiar rowdy roar behind me. As both eternity and the end of the hallway approached, I turned to start down the stairs. One last time I expectantly glanced down the hall toward the conference room. A cannon shot could be fired from one end of the hall to the other and no harm would be done.

I haltingly descended the two flights of marble stairs as if disappearing into a dense fog. Filled with what had just taken place, I was oblivious to my surroundings. I exited the north entrance of this east wing of University Hospital and mechanically crossed the hospital lawn, the four-lane street out front, and worked my way through the VA Hospital's parking lot, which delivered me at the steps of the loading dock that formed an apron next to the back entrance of the VA Hospital.

During this fog-like transition from one campus to the other, I contemplated rather weighty thoughts such as, "Will this be my last day of this residency program?" "Will I be black-balled from all my programs in the future?" "How will I pay the rent and feed my family without my stipend?"

In my mind's eye, I hurriedly reflected through the process of contemplating my assignment, my decision to abort that assignment, and then every detail of my substituted dissertation. I was supposed to prepare and deliver a learned clinical discussion — appropriate, timely and informative to each person in attendance. However, my current residency responsibilities seemed to be both too demanding and time-consuming to allow adequate study and preparation. The more I thought about the plight of all first-year residents, the more frustrated I became and the more I wanted to speak out. I wrestled within myself concerning what I wanted to say versus what I needed to do in preparation to deliver the expected talk.

Then on Thursday, I had an unbelievably and horrendously busy day and night as "medical officer of the day." Simultaneously, a letter arrived from a referring primary care physician. This doctor's comments sealed my decision.

I am sure that I did not hear a word the first speaker uttered. When I was called upon, I got up and went to the front of the room. I paused a moment, looking at the chief of medicine, all of the staff members, residents, interns, medical students and a smattering of nurses, took a big breath and began.

Essence of My Dissertation

I apologize to you, but with your forbearance, and in lieu of my assigned topic, I would like to share with you some deep concerns I have about our training program.

While attending medical school at this university, I was impressed that the internal medicine program was one that shared a healthy blend of hands-on clinical experience, adequate time for in-depth study of disease entities and the luxury of being exposed to the wisdom of the excellent staff in this department.

Comfortable with this program, and having received confirmation of a position in this residency program, I elected to apply for a rotating internship where I would spend a year in a "shoot-'em-up" environment: the Kansas City General Hospital, an institution long on trauma, all the responsibility one could stand and, in essence, a "learning by doing" experience.

I expected this rotating internship to be in stark contrast to, and ideally a preparation for, the internal medicine program I would return to this year. When I arrived here in July, program changes had been made to make residency years two and three more appealing. They have indeed done so. Rotating through the clinics with neither call nor primary ward responsibilities is indeed a plum for those beyond year one. However, in doing this, it has made some of the first-year rotations a hazing-like nightmare.

When we are on call at the VA, we cover three medical wards plus the neurology ward. We must respond to nursing calls from all four wards, and one must give new orders and check patients for any clinical concerns that may arise. We must evaluate and determine the disposition of every patient who comes to the emergency room. After 5 p.m. we must go to the lab and microscopically confirm the appropriateness of every unit of blood typed and cross-matched by the lab technician on call.

After 7 p.m. we are given the keys to the pharmacy. When, for one reason or another, an additional medication is needed on the medical or surgical wards, we must find, label and dispense that medication.

At 10 p.m. the EKG technician goes home. We must personally run and interpret the EKGs for the entire hospital. We must receive all admissions that arrive from local referrals, as well as those from out-state. We must respond to all code blues and run those codes. If the patient expires, we must make the pronouncement, take care of necessary notifications and be responsible for appropriate certification, as well as to establish a time for a critique of that code, including all who participated.

I was on call yesterday. During the course of the day and evening I had nine admissions. Of those admitted last evening, one gentleman had an acute myocardial infarction (MI). Another gentleman came as a reported congestive heart failure (CHF). On the patient's arrival, the medical student was impressed with his cardiovascular findings.

After but a brief encounter, I found from the patient's history that he was having florid black (melena) stools. An emergency complete blood count (CBC) revealed a hemoglobin of 6 grams (normal 12 to 16 grams). The medical student spent most of the night irrigating the nasogastric tube with ice water while we transfused him to tide him over for a surgical consultation this morning.

While trying to assess and care for the remainder of the new admissions, pages continued to come from the other wards for both routine and not-so-routine orders and assessments. Throughout the night I remained, on average, four responses behind in my ability to keep up with my pages.

In the back of my mind remained the haunting fact that a pile of charts perched in my call room awaited review, discharge summaries and letters to referring physicians. At times, this stack of charts begging completion has been two to three feet deep.

There are currently 55 patients on my ward at the VA Hospital. A high percent of these patients have serious illnesses. This week, two of my patients died. It is expected that we attend the autopsy of those patients in the event there may still be something further which would be instructive regarding the patient's illness. In lieu of that responsibility, I sent the medical students and continued working on the ward. My staff physician called me into his office specifically to express his concern about my not being present at the autopsies.

I rather vehemently responded, "The patients are being admitted so rapidly I can do little more than triage. I feel that my first obligation is to those patients who are living. I can't do anything further for those who are dead!"

Paperwork

Due to the pace on the ward, I have fallen far behind on my paperwork and particularly the discharge summaries, as I mentioned. More importantly, however, are the letters to referring physicians. Let me read you the letter I just received:

Dear Dr. Hahn,

You'll recall that I referred my patient, Mr. Very Sick, to you approximately five weeks ago. He has since been evaluated and treated by you and your staff. He appears to have made a dramatic recovery and returned home two and a half weeks ago. When he came to the office today, he reported that you had studied him from stem to stern. He is now on a whole new regime of medications and feels like he is doing very well. My hat is off to your good care.

However, to date I have not received one piece of correspondence from you or your institution. Those of us who practice in smaller communities around the state depend on you and your colleagues at University for not only the sophisticated laboratory services and high-powered consultations, but for the part you play in our continuing education.

Indeed, the summary of your evaluation, findings and recommendations are very important for the care of our individual patients such as Mr. Very Sick. We base our continued care for Mr. Sick on those recommendations. Perhaps even more im-

portant to us, however, is the update which you give us regarding various disease entities, what tests are available for appropriate assessment and current thinking on medications and treatments.

For those of us who do not get to the University or to meetings very often, you are responsible for providing our continuing medical education. I know that you are busy. I'm busy, too! So is Mr. Phelps down at the corner pharmacy and Mr. Smith at the hardware store. I trust that I will hear from you very soon!

Sincerely,
I Am Ticked, M.D.

In summary, I feel that we first-year residents are not receiving the educational opportunity which we anticipated and for which we contracted. Secondly, we are not able to provide for either our patients or our referring physicians in a manner that is professionally appropriate. Thank you, or excuse me, whichever the case may be.

Exit Stage Left

I arrived at the back dock of the VA Hospital oblivious to the many steps I had taken across the University Hospital campus, the four-lane street, and the VA parking lot. Reaching the dock entrance shook me back into the reality of my remaining ward responsibilities. These begged my attention before my conscience would allow me to go home. Each of us on the VA rotation stayed on at the end of the day to clear up any specific ward problems that might make it easier for the doctor on call to survive.

This particular Friday evening, there were even more lab reports to be checked, intravenous fluids and medicine orders to be written and paperwork details to be accomplished than on the usual non-call night. It was fully 9 p.m. before I finally looked up from my work, comfortable that things would be okay until the following day.

Not until I took the elevator from the third to the first floor, walked back across the loading dock, down its half flight of concrete steps, and was well on the way to my parking space did my mind once more return to my unprecedented outburst at the conference and, in fact, that my longevity as a medical resident was in jeopardy.

I again mulled over my conference room antics on the 12-minute drive home. As I pulled into the garage, my thoughts jumped to what I would tell Marge about the day's events.

To my surprise, she met me at the kitchen door. Before I could begin to reconstruct the happenings of the day, she hastily volunteered that Dr. Ian Smith had called, gave her some sense of what had gone on, and then told her to pass on to me that he was both appreciative of my comments and supportive of my forthrightness to speak out at the conference. He further informed her that Dr. Bean had called a special department meeting Saturday morning to reconsider various aspects of the residency program.

Needless to say, I was profoundly relieved by Dr. Smith's call as I retraced the events of the day for Marge. I felt even further exonerated by the fact that I was still at the hospital at 8:15 p.m. on a non-call night when Dr. Smith attempted to reach me. That night I rested better than I had for weeks and perhaps months.

Saturday morning I contacted a senior peer in the program. He was a chief resident and had been at the conference. He said, "When you finished and left the room, everyone sat there like they were in a state of shock. Fully two minutes passed with not one person getting up or speaking. Then Dr. Bean stood up from his usual position on the front row, turned around to those in attendance, and asked, 'How do the rest of you feel about Dr. Hahn's comments?' "

With Dr. Bean's invitation, other first-year residents hesitantly and cautiously began to vent similar feelings. As they came to appreciate Dr. Bean's genuine concern and openness, they expanded on their personal experiences in this difficult situation.

The advanced residents, although pleased with their present situation, confirmed my concerns and granted that it had been difficult enough for them previously when first- and second-year residents had shared ward responsibilities and call.

A full half-hour passed before Dr. Bean called the discussion to a close and assured those present that the matter would be promptly taken under advisement.

The next morning the medical department staff did meet. The program was changed immediately with due consideration given to the first-year residents.

Despite the fact that we were close to the end of the year and that I left the program at the end of that year in favor of a surgical specialty residency in ENT at the Mayo Graduate School of Medicine, I always had the highest regard for both Dr. Smith and Dr. Bean.

Dr. Smith was the classic kind and thoughtful mentor whose primary expertise was research in infectious disease. At the same time, he was a knowledgeable teacher in all aspects of medicine.

Through the remainder of the year, Dr. Bean continued to treat me with the utmost respect, despite my comments and my announced ultimate decision to leave his program to go into ENT. I'll always appreciate the opportunity I had to spend a year in his internal medicine program under his extraordinary tutelage. I was further appreciative of being heard as that one voice crying out in the wilderness who was allowed to effect a constructive alteration in the residency program.

▪ CHAPTER 27 ▪

The Art of Being Tuned In

MANY SERMONS HAVE focused on looking beyond our-selves — beyond our personal dreams, hopes, and aspirations — and directing our energies toward doing those things that would benefit others. Today, when I hear a sermon like that, I remember back to my Mayo ENT residency when I was deeply impressed by a resident peer's concern for others. We'll call him "Dr. Nick."

My fellow resident, Dr. Nick, openly acknowledged being less adept and less interested in developing the manual dexter-ity required for surgery than his ENT residency classmates. He did, however, exhibit a genuine concern for his patients' non-surgical needs. With great patience, he would listen to a patient's less-than-abbreviated list of concerns and symptoms and respond appropriately. Dr. Nick's personal patterns or id-iosyncrasies did mean that he handled fewer patient visits than the rest of us; however, these same traits often proved advanta-geous for his patients.

With this mindset, Dr. Nick rotated just ahead of me to one of four routine training sites which we then referred to as the "state hospital." The majority of patients here came from other state institutions (handicapped, psychiatric and penal) for medical and surgical needs.

There were patients with a variety of psychiatric diagnoses. For example, one short-term trustworthy patient had an ex-tremely obsessive-compulsive personality. This fellow often greeted me in the main corridor of the hospital as he walked with a hand continuously in contact with the wall. To avoid breaking physical contact with a wall, he walked into every cove and side hallway as he progressed toward his destination.

Another memorable day, while working my way through the patient list at the state hospital clinic, I came upon a young lady in her teens who spoke with a whispered voice and complained of being "hoarse." This type of voice is typical of an entity called "hysteric dysphonia." It is a functional problem rather than a physical one. The diagnosis was confirmed when I had her protrude her tongue, held a mirror in her pharynx (between her tonsils) and looked indirectly down at her vocal cords. Her vocal cords were normal color, moved well, and produced a normal "A" sound when asked to phonate that sound. However, after the mirror exam she resumed her whispered speaking voice, convinced she had a physical ailment.

A little light bulb came on in my head. I took a topical anesthetic spray bottle and sprayed a couple of puffs against the back of her throat (that only caused brief topical anesthesia). I suggested to the young lady that in a short time the spray would cause her to speak normally. She then left the office. Ten minutes later the nurse on the ward called asking how we had "cured" the girl's voice problem. That day we didn't solve the young lady's psychiatric problems, but we did document her acute diagnosis and reversed those symptoms.

Severe mentally or physically handicapped (in-house) patients were often bedfast. Others were placed in wheelchairs and held in place by sheets wrapped around them and tied behind the back of the chair. Those who could communicate in some form were periodically pushed into the day room to gain whatever they could from fraternization. Here, at least, nonverbal contact could be made through the mere presence of other patients.

At the other end of the spectrum, inmates from both the male and female penal institutions were transferred for medical or surgical assistance. Some were trustees; others, dangerous inmates, moving about in handcuffs and leg chains with an armed guard at their elbow.

After evening meals, ambulatory patients and those in wheelchairs were taken to the day room where recreational therapists provided games, puzzles, books and appropriate assistance for those not engrossed in television. The personal attention given to these inmates, coupled with the tender loving care of the nursing staff, made the stay for most patients well worth the procedural or surgical discomfort inmates might have to endure.

Removal of an Eraser

I particularly recall one teenage boy (we'll call "Sam") who was moderately retarded. He was admitted to the state hospital at least two times in the course of my three-month rotation. My first encounter with Sam occurred when he wedged a rubber eraser from the end of a pencil into his ear canal. The staff at his institution could not dislodge it, so he was sent to the state hospital for a brief general anesthesia and minor procedure. This simply required using a fine surgical right angle hook and an operating microscope to remove the eraser. By handling the problem in this gentle manner, Sam experienced no pain and at the same time enjoyed three days of R&R away from his primary institution. In fact, the trip was so enjoyable that he repeated the eraser trick a number of times.

Sam seemed to space his visits at long enough intervals that they did not become excessively annoying to anyone. If the surgery suite was crowded or a weekend intervened, he received two or more "bonus" days. This pattern just might indicate that he was a bit less retarded than most professionals thought. Finally realizing his strategy, we elected to carry out the removal without anesthesia and with modest discomfort. To no one's surprise, Sam did not repeat the feat.

It was during such extended stays in what appeared to be a similar patient that Dr. Nick made an outstanding observation (let's call the patient "Herb"). Some of the more astute male patients were putting a large puzzle together on a card table. Herb, who was thought to be deaf and severely retarded, stood by the table watching the men working on the puzzle while Dr. Nick stood nearby observing the activities. To Dr. Nick's astonishment, Herb would quite frequently lean over, pick up and position a piece of the puzzle the other patients had been seeking for some time. The "retarded" label immediately came under suspicion in my friend's mind.

With this reprogramming of conceptions, Dr. Nick began to wonder about the nature of the lad's deafness. Herb had bilateral congenital ear malformations (microtia and atresia — small ears with no external ear canals). His only communication was an occasional burst of non-intelligible guttural sounds mixed with screeches. Dr. Nick's curiosity was now stimulated. He acquired a bone conduction hearing aid and began feeding Herb a barrage of amplified elementary information at the grade level of an early preschooler. Testing of this totally undisciplined lad at this point was not reliable, but there appeared to be significant cochlear (hearing) reserve. Further attention, time and concerned dedication of many staff members led to early efforts by Herb to mimic the sounds of colors, numbers and body parts (not unlike the techniques Dr. Nick used in teaching his own children).

This encouragement led to a more complete evaluation, X-rays and eventual surgery to establish external ear canals for Herb. The boy's demeanor and direction in life became progressively more purposeful. He followed the nurses and anyone else who would feed his starved appetite for learning. Herb's meaningless outbreaks of frustrated noise abated, and his whole demeanor became one of interest and purpose. When I rotated off the service, Herb was accurately carrying out the verbal exchanges one would see in a preschooler.

I am not privy to the number of family members, friends, medical personnel, friends of the courts or institutional employees whom Dr. Nick has impacted. Likewise, I do not know the outcome of Herb's adult years. But I do know that Dr. Nick's interest and concern, followed by his dedication to satisfy this young person's needs, did change Herb's life from the boredom of intellectual isolation to the joy of expanded pathways of learning.

Today, we in medicine join the rest of the world in looking for "the quick fix." Too many physicians are guilty of consulting without touching the patient or "taking their hand off the examining room doorknob." In so doing, practitioners may miss some of the most rewarding outcomes for both their patients and themselves.

■ CHAPTER 28 ■

The Art of Maturing in Medicine

IN THE PROCESS of teaching "younger" medical professionals, I repeatedly tell them, "The only way to mature in medicine is to grow older. Experience what one can in a day, but maturing requires many days."

First experiences in health care are uniformly a bit tenuous and insecure. Similarly, "patients" first experiencing medical care are tainted with a degree of anxiety and fearful anticipation of the care they will receive.

Communicating

Preceding my junior year of medical school, I worked on the men's medical ward at the State University of Iowa hospitals as a Medical Nurse Assistant (MNA — glorified orderly). My assignment included taking admission vitals, recording basic health information and doing minor care services for patients on the ward.

One day a 23-year-old single male, clearly from "the farm" and as spooked as a deer in the headlights of a car, sat anxiously on the edge of his bed as I entered the room. He had just been admitted to the floor for a medical workup. He had donned his "semi-private" gown over his shorts and waited expectantly as I approached him with my stethoscope around my neck, the three-foot-high metal floor-standing blood pressure machine and an old-fashioned glass thermometer in my shirt pocket.

In those days, glass thermometers came in two configurations. Each was approximately five inches long with a mercury bulb at the bottom end. One was an oral thermometer that had a narrowed bottom end about one half inch long. The other, a rectal thermometer, had a slightly thickened bulbous end approximately one-quarter of an inch in length. On the medicine wards, oral thermometers were considered less accurate. Therefore, all temperatures were taken rectally.

After taking the young man's pulse and blood pressure and asking him about any allergies and use of daily medicines, I explained that I needed to take his temperature. I further explained that on this ward, temperatures were taken rectally. I then asked, "Would you like to put it in yourself or do you want me to put it in?" He quickly grunted, "I will." Nervously, he grabbed it from my outstretched hand and stuck it in his mouth.

Just as quickly, I said, "No, no, rectally!" Even more quickly he pulled it out of his mouth, turned it around and put the other end in his mouth. Again, I nicely said," No, this goes in your other end."

"Oh, in my ass," he blurted out. (This should not be as distasteful as it sounds as the thermometers, once used, were washed with soap and water, then cold sterilized in a disinfectant and "spun down" in a centrifuge before reusing them.)

New learning experiences, whether initiating or receiving, begin in just this manner.

This young man was in a private room because of the suspicion of his having a contagious GI tract infection. Nonetheless, I still dispensed the thermometers and took routine vitals on him just as I did on everyone else on the ward.

New Experiences

On another day, I was going down one side of the ward and coming back the other, inserting or handing out thermometers for patients to insert themselves. I started across the front of the ward to collect thermometers distributed five minutes earlier, in the same order they were distributed. As I did so, I would record the temperatures on a chart. I also took and recorded the patients' pulse and blood pressure.

As I crossed back to the side of the room where I first distributed the thermometers, I heard a tinkle typical of breaking glass, followed by a thud. As I looked around, the first man who received his thermometer had dropped his thermometer on the polished concrete floor, fallen from his chair and lay slumped and motionless on the floor. I gave an immediate cry for help. The resident and intern were there instantaneously, resuscitated the fellow, who was about 50 years of age, and provided me with my first experience of seeing someone literally dead and brought back to life.

He was moved to the intensive care ward, once his heart rate, blood pressure and consciousness returned. Days later, he returned to our ward, seemingly "little worse for wear" and with no recollection of the incident at all.

Hands-on experiences are maturing experiences. Just assisting the bedfast patients onto bedpans, distributing urinals, and "cleaning up" these patients is one more step along the educational chain.

Patient Expectations

The "men's" wards were more like "old boys' clubs." The "walking wounded" freely cared for each others' needs, whether it be getting fresh water, pulling the privacy curtains or emptying a urinal for someone who could not do so for themselves.

When I rotated onto the "women's" wards, there was generally very little camaraderie. "The girls" usually were more private and expectant of hands-on care from the orderlies, aids and nurses.

I still recall one rather obese older woman who motioned for me to come to her bed. She pulled her gown up to her neck and shoulders, took one of her heavy breasts with both hands and, holding it suspended toward her head, whined, "Honey, it's all galled under here. Would you put some powder on it?" And so I did (another new experience!).

Risks

Another time, a young man was admitted to the ward who was markedly jaundiced from hepatitis. The various varieties of hepatitis were not well defined at that point, and the major thrust was clarifying the cause as to whether the patient had a stone in the common bile duct, a malignancy at the head of the pancreas, or indeed the then defined hepatitis "A" or "B."

Maturing in medicine includes realizing that there is risk in caring for the sick (in this case, jaundiced). Those in health care have the additional burden of patient care despite innate risks.

I also delivered food trays to this young man and collected them on a regular basis. I then took the trays to a decontamination area. In doing cares within the room, I gowned and put on a mask and gloves as carefully as I knew how.

However, that fall I had bacteriology as one of my second-year medical school courses. The professor was a virologist who, by coincidence, was studying hepatitis. In fact, he drew a blood sample from all of his class members who were willing to contribute a sample. I was one of the two or three in the class who had a very high titer for hepatitis. As I recall, my titer was quoted as 1:1300.

This made me special! I was invited to contribute a pint of blood, which at that time was used to furnish immunoglobulins to treat others who had been exposed to hepatitis. For this deed, I was given a $50 fee per pint (reward). This was a significant sum of money for one who made only a couple of dollars per hour working as an MNA.

Night Shift — Advanced Expectations

Finding competent help for nursing staff during the night-time hours is often a challenge. Realizing this, one of the mechanisms of an assured place to work is volunteering for the nightshift.

Early on, in truly "open-heart" (bypass surgery is "open chest" surgery but not open heart surgery) surgery, Dr. Aaronhof was the head of the Department of Cardiac Surgery at the University of Iowa. One of the conditions he operated on was a congenital septal defect in a little lad eight years of age. He was a darling, polite little boy who suffered one of the complications of open heart surgery before the technology of cardiac pacemakers had arrived on the scene.

During his surgical repair, the Bundle of His was compromised. It was believed that this electrical system responsible for the rhythmic contraction of the heart was damaged in repairing his septal defect. This led to the situation where multiple times during the course of a day the young man would have a cardiac arrest.

I was hired as a "special" to work the nightshift. My task was to sit by the boy's side for eight hours. Each time his heart stopped, I would push the buzzer for the charge nurse, clear any contact with the metal bed, and use the Ambu bag to ventilate him until the nurse arrived. When she came, I would grab the electrical paddles, place one over his heart and one on his lateral chest, prepared for the nurse to trigger the defibrillator and restart his heart.

During his waking hours he was fully alert and cooperative. We visited about subjects that would be of interest to any primary schoolboy. On one of the shifts I shocked him eight times. This process went on around the clock for a number of days. Twenty-three defibrillation efforts were conducted before his tired little body gave out. Again, this was in a time frame when pacemakers and implantable defibrillators had not been invented. Fortunately for the sake of my own "heart," he passed away on a daytime shift when I was not on duty.

ER

During my rotating internship year, I had two daughters in early primary school. My stipend of $300 per month was not enough to clothe, feed and house the family, and have enough money to transport myself to and from General Hospital located in downtown Kansas City, Missouri. In those days, it was common for residents and interns to man emergency rooms in the local hospitals. This not only supplemented the inadequate stipend, but furnished further maturing in medical experience and judgment.

Early in my internship year I was able to find a "moonlighting" job in the emergency room at the Independence Sanitarium and Hospital (ISH). This was the only hospital in eastern Jackson County, Missouri at that time. It was convenient as we rented a duplex only 10 blocks away. Here, an intern or resident would arrive at the emergency room at 5:30 or 6 p.m., when the doctors in the offices nearby closed shop for the day. At this hour, the routine clinics and operating room would close as well.

We ER physicians were basically the only physician in the hospital from 6 p.m. until 6 a.m. the next day, except for the OB doctors who came and went at all hours. We did everything from sewing up lacerations to treating Strep throats. We provided initial care for fractures, as well as triaging more serious medical problems, such as acute myocardial infarctions, severe gastrointestinal tract problem, and the delivery of babies when the OB had not yet arrived.

When a series of injuries such as the bad auto accident came in, we were the only doctor available to do triage until an appropriate hospital staff physician(s) could be contacted and arrive.

I recall one early morning I sewed for hours on a man's face that had gone through a windshield. During the course of this repair, I had to pause multiple times to take care of less serious medical complaints.

One of the most demanding episodes was an auto accident with five of the patients literally in shock and occupying all of the gurneys in this small ER, while others waited in the hallway to be seen.

IVs were started with large bore needles (15 gauge) to administer fluids at a rate that would keep the patient's blood pressure in an acceptable range until the surgeon arrived and took them to the operating room, or administered other appropriate care.

While in the midst of this chaotic situation being managed by yours truly, the night nurse supervisor received a call from the ambulance company. There had been another wreck about seven miles away, and they were on their way with two more patients.

As I later thought to myself, it was fortunate that the two boys in the Corvette who launched over a 50- to 100-foot embankment landing in a field were actually dead, as I had no place to care for them had they been alive.

One creepy note was that one of the two boys had literally been partially decapitated. The crown of his head had been sheared off just above the eyebrow, as sharply as if he had been hit with a machete. His skull was completely empty of brain tissue. Perhaps an hour and a half later, two men came to the ER carrying a chambray shirt with the lad's brain wrapped up inside. For what purpose, I'm not sure.

On another occasion, while in the same ER, I was called emergently to the delivery suite where a pregnant lady without any prenatal care was forwarded from the reception desk in full labor. The baby had proceeded to crown and was ready for delivery. As I delivered the baby, it was completely flaccid, never demonstrating any muscle tone or effort to breathe. I intubated the baby and ventilated it with an Ambu bag while the nurse contacted the obstetrician on call. He suggested appropriate stimulants to be used in an effort to get the child to respond. All of our efforts failed, and the sluggish weak heart rate diminished and disappeared.

In further exploring the mother's history after the child died, we found that she had previously delivered five children. Only one of those survived. The remainder were flaccid babies who never responded to neonatal efforts similar to those that we instituted. Why the woman would not seek prenatal care having been faced with this history was beyond our understanding.

Maturing Through Error

One evening an inebriated young man came in from an auto accident. He had an extensive forehead and scalp laceration, but was conscious. This was long before CAT scans and MRIs had arrived on the market.

I did call a general surgeon because, in my estimation, the patient had an associated "acute abdomen." I elicited "rebound" (a momentary sharp discomfort when one pushes steadily on the abdomen and then releases quickly). I also observed that his abdomen was silent (no bowel sounds). The general surgeon disagreed with my findings in the abdomen and sent the patient to the floor after his facial and scalp laceration repair had been carried out under local anesthesia.

I later heard through the grapevine my next time on call that the young man had indeed bled out into his abdomen and died later that same evening he was admitted.

Doctors do make judgment errors, though it may have been more likely before all of the diagnostic tools we have available today.

Sharing Grief Is Maturing

Elderly patients are commonly brought to the ER for pronouncement, or when they have arrived at an agonal state (their last moments of dying). The family is receptive and expectant in most of these cases. However, when it is a youth, or unexpected, it becomes a difficult situation for both the doctor and the patient's family.

Such a case was that of a 10-year-old child. He was working with his father in the garage when a neighbor boy came for help to get his ball out of a culvert next to the road. The father gave the boys a piece of cardboard that had been laying in the garage and suggested one of the boys lie on this as he reached into the culvert to get the ball. In this way, he would not get wet and muddy.

While the man's son was lying in the ditch on the cardboard and reaching for the ball, a mail truck slipped off the edge of the blacktop on the opposite side of the narrow street, over-corrected and came back across the street, into the ditch and right across the young man's chest as he lay on the cardboard in the ditch.

He was brought to the emergency room unconscious, bubbling frothy blood from his mouth and nostrils and making minimal chest efforts to breathe. I quickly intubated him and put him on a Byrd respirator, which was the state-of-the-art ventilator at that time. His chance of survival in those days was essentially zero, and it would be unlikely that he would have had a much better chance of survival even with today's technology.

He was the only son in the family with three sisters. Chaplain Don Harvey came to be with the family as I told the boy's mother, father and sisters that "he was gone."

Maturing in medicine includes wanting to weep with the family, but professionally not being allowed to do so. These experiences were each distance markers on the road to maturity in medicine.

■ CHAPTER 29 ■

The Art of Looking Back

AFTER YEARS OF experiencing, learning, growing and preparing, one at the end of a classic medical education has a chance to look back before stepping onto that treadmill which will hopefully lead to years of professional productivity.

All of life before this moment, cumulatively determines who one is and how they will meet the challenges that lie before them. Life's experiences to this point provide confidence, understanding and direction to meet those needs in the lives of patients who seek their "doctor" for medical advice and care. Each medical practitioner is the product of a given pathway of preparation. I humbly feel that all those seeking health care deserve to thoroughly understand the nature of the preparation and the credentials of the "doctors" they select.

It is further my belief that persons should have the right to choose their "doctor." However, the tax-supported health care system should ONLY be financially responsible for those "doctors" and modalities of care that have been academically demonstrated to give reliable and proven results.

In my opinion, alternative methods of health care should *only* be expensed to society *after* being subjected to such accumulative documentation as rendered by reproducible outcomes and appropriately administered double-blind studies.

Anecdotal reports furnished by those wishing to circumvent scientific methods should *not* be allowed to turn the heads of uninformed legislators through highly paid lobbyists and politically and financially motivated backing.

We know that approximately 30 percent of all patients will respond to the Placebo Effect (sugar pill). This fact lends itself to those who have incurable illnesses, those with hypochondriacal tendencies, those who cannot afford mainstream medicine and those who are just plain medically naive. Collectively, this leads to a large segment of our population falling prey to soothsayers and charlatans.

Our financially struggling health care system can ill afford this waste of health care dollars. Even more disconcerting is the fact that many patients with serious or life-threatening illnesses can waste both time and financial means in search of non-existent panaceas.

It goes without saying, there are those of us in classical Western medicine who have less than high ethical standards. There are those of us not willing to make the necessary effort to stay current. And there are others of us who do make mistakes typical of all human beings. This being said, I firmly believe that the Doctorate in Medicine (M.D.) and the practice of medicine demands both the highest ethical and academic *standards* of the professions. A continuous effort to decrease the number of errors is a given.

My challenge to my peers is to constantly reach toward those goals.

My challenge to society is to be informed and not to be lured into the trap of ill-advised and anecdotally supported health care misadventures.

My challenge to our legislative bodies and judicial divisions is to uphold the honesty, trust and standard of ethics we should expect from *everyone* in our society.